Kirsten N

MW01536350

Not to Talk About
Until Now

By
Kirsten Marie Wohlgemuth
kwohlg@gmail.com

This book may not be reproduced in any
form without the permission of the publisher

Copyright 2014

Kirsten Marie Wohlgemuth
All Rights Reserved

ISBN - 13:978-1493598410
ISBN -10:1493598414

Printed in the United States of America

Thank you to all who helped me to completion:
My proofreaders;
Carolyn T., Rita P., Betty T., Kathy B.H., Chris H.

With the guiding and sharing at *Write On the edge,*
A writers' group in Yuma, Arizona,
The story has unfolded.

I am proud of my perseverance.

I have one other novel

'Among The Flowers'

To my dear Diane (65th)
When I'm with you
I feel at home!

2 *All my love*
Kris

Authors Note

The job of writing this has taken 28 years. When I began in 1986 with pen and paper it was a form of therapy for me. At that time I had no idea about the ending or the in between. As life unfolded, my story grew. It has helped me along the way to get the sadness down on paper because as someone once said to me 'You can't talk that way,' even if it was the truth. People want to hear pleasantries, happy stories about happy lives. Writing has given this author the freedom to say it all.

At first I thought the genre of my book would be 'Young Adult.' There are strong messages to young adults about taking charge of your life, avoiding the many pitfalls of substance abuse in today's society, and making good decisions or suffering the unthinkable consequences. Living in an alcoholic home is tough.

Adults should also read this book. Think of prevention or change for yourself, for family members. Rehabilitate—Recognize the signs. Above all—communicate—make it—

Something to Talk About

Kirsten Marie Wohlgemuth

a mother on her back

 a new generation emerges

to view the world

dandelion fluff

a new mother caresses

her baby's head

By

Carmel Hayes Westerman,

 member of the Haiku Society of America

and an Inspirational Poet and Novelist of:

Mrs. Atwater; Anna May; Bessie's Story.

Kirsten Marie Wohlgemuth

Not to Talk About

Until Now

Kirsten Marie Wohlgemuth
Author

CHAPTER 1
Denmark 1985

She spent that morning fussing with her nails, hair, and makeup—not too much, just enough—an outfit, not too fancy, not too casual. Above all, she wants to feel comfortable and not end up fidgeting with some detail of her ensemble.

*****

Her entire body trembled. Tears threatened as she stood in front of the double door of the large, yellow brick house, with a flat roof. It was different from most Danish red brick houses but, it was impressive.

The varnished door shone and its brass doorknob and hinges gleamed in the sunlight.

Thirty five years, all of her life from the time her mind began wondering and searching, Kirsten dreamt of, fantasized about, wished, hoped, and prayed for this moment. Her pulse banged in her ears and her breath was shallow. *I am standing at the door to my father's home. Oh my GOD, this is the entry to his life! S*he rang the doorbell. They were about to meet face to face, for the first time.

The time between the ringing of the doorbell and the door opening, seemed like an eternity. *Will I in some way be forever changed when I leave through this door? Will I see myself in him? What is going through my father's mind?*

CHAPTER 2
Denmark 1949

With signed paternity papers in place, Ava felt somewhat relieved. The son-of-a- bitch owned up to fathering her bastard. After Christian refused to marry, she had gone to his parents, and told them they could expect a grandchild.

Everyone in this city knows we have more than most," Were you intentionally planning to trap our son?" asked Christian's father.

"Think what you will. There was no planning anything. I can't afford to raise your grandchild on my own. If you don't want messy stories circulating around town may I suggest you use your influence on Christian. See that I get what is needed," said Ava.
They agreed to pay the support if he would not. Ava wanted more than Christian, himself. She needed security too.

Christian owned up to paternity and agreed to pay child support. He would soon go to Copenhagen, serve in the King's Royal Guard, and flee the situation of their short lived romance—a few dances, a little drinking, heavy necking and petting, followed by a one night stand of consensual sex on a blanket behind the dance hall.

*****

Ava lay in her grandmother's bed, upstairs in a cramped bedroom, of the small red brick house. She was

7

laboring into her second day. Her grandmother was the midwife in the small community of Ostervedsted, and had her opinion about her headstrong granddaughter, "at twenty four years old, you should have known not to get in the family way," she chided.

"Don't give me your wisdom lecture…Ahh crap the misery of this….Ahh that son of a bitch!" Ava screamed "I hate him! I hate him!" *Ahh he will pay, oh yes he will pay! Damn it, Christian will not get his hands on this child. He didn't want me so he will never, ever, see the baby.*

*****

As an experienced midwife, Ava's grandmother worried. This labor was lasting too long and worried about her great grandchild. She felt excited and happy as always to help at a birth--new life, such a miracle, but sometimes it went wrong. This time was different—she was personally and emotionally involved—her first great grandbaby on the way.

"Wilhelm, you may have to fetch the doctor soon if the child takes much longer," she shouted at her husband from the bottom of the stairway.

Ava's scream for help was heard throughout the house loud and clear. Wilhelm winced with worry for his great grandchild trapped inside during such a long labor. He shooed his wife back up the stairs.

"Wife, go quick, go now. Maybe it's time. GOD be with us all!" He went to his chair grabbed for his long pipe and rocked in time with the tick tock of the clock. *I will wait. If she yells one more time I'll fetch the Doc. We might not need him.*

*****

"Ahh, grandma help me please!" She screamed and twisted her body. *I feel as if a dull knife is cutting through my backbone—damn it!*

"Good girl, Ava, keep pushing. You can do it. A little rest…now, push some more." Panting, screaming, and sweating, Ava pushed the infant down the birth canal.

The baby's bald head crowned, "come on little one, come on now." *I am about to meet my first great grandchild. Please Lord let everything be all right.* Soon, the shoulders emerged. The newborn appeared lifeless—a grey blue color. Ava stayed silent while her Grandmother prepared to cut the cord. A slight mewling sound came from the infant followed by a hearty cry as her little body flushed a healthy pink.

"Well, Grandma, your Great Granddaughter will be named after you. Her name, like yours, is Kirsten Marie. Please can I get some sleep? I know you will have fun doing whatever it is that you do for newborns."

Burping, bathing, and cuddling was done by Ava's Grandmother, Kirsten, her mother, Emma, or one of Ava's sisters. Breastfeeding, Ava had to do but she was quick to hand her over anytime someone was willing to take her.

*****

Ava found a job as a housekeeper and cook for a widowed, older gentleman, Jens Nonneker. Room and board was included for both her and baby, Kirsten. It was a spacious, two stories, and white board house with a beautiful garden. Kirsten charmed the old man and he loved spending time with her.

"Oh Ava, little Kis crawled today when I rolled the ball on the lawn," said Nonneker.

"You said Kis? Her name is Kirsten."

"She is Kis to me." Her pet name stuck until she started school.

CHAPTER 3

Please come, somebody hurry, hurry and come! Three years old, Kis awakened in the early grey dawn, and found herself alone in the bed she shared with her mother. She toddled off of the sofa bed, paused on the cold wood floor of the sleeping/sitting room and peeked into the only other room in the tiny apartment—the kitchen, which also served as a bathroom, a pail for a toilet.

Kis did her pee then shivered as she pitter-pattered the short distance to the front window and quietly began to weep. She climbed onto a scratchy, cane bottom chair and peered outside to the narrow street of uneven cobblestones. All that greeted her there was a fine mist of rain and dull sky—no sign of her Mum, not even Mum's bike. When her breath fogged up the pane, she rubbed the window, straining to peer further out. Her tummy rumbled and she went in search of food. She reached the sugar bowl and pacified herself with 2 big scoops, and then returned to the window on tip toes.

Kis recognized familiar sounds of footsteps. She bounced up and down, clapped her hands and jumped into the arms of the old man, Ib Ibsen, who heard her moving about. He and Mrs. Ibsen owned the house in which Kis and her mother lived. In his arms, the little girl pointed at an imaginary, buzzing bee as she babbled on. Ib rocked her while he hummed a melody. Sometimes she stayed with the Ibsens in their part of the house and loved the cozy, peaceful, atmosphere. Mrs. Ibsen's sausage and mashed potatoes with brown gravy was tasty. Ib liked to read to Kis who listened and later tried to retell the story back to him. She beamed with pride when they praised her to Ava.

*****

"Tomorrow you will go around the corner, to Mrs. Jensen and her brats. Those softies next door have spoiled you enough," Ava said.

At Mrs. Jensen's, who had her own four kids and two others, she babysat. It was survival of the fittest. Kis endured spittle in her face, hair pulling, biting, and shoving to the ground, among other frustrating acts to establish one's position.

There were good things too, like the time an older kid found a bit of chewing gum on the sidewalk.

"Look here, lucky me, look what I found, bet you all wish it were yours! Here, Kis, you can have it!" The others clapped and laughed. Kis closed her eyes, and opened her mouth as instructed. Triumphant, she chomped down on the cold, pre-chewed, tough offering.

The worst was bedding down for the night—a miserable struggle—four kids to a single bed, two at each end. There was always a tug of war with the feather comforter. Feet kicked all over the place. Stinky farts exploded, followed by malicious laughter, and billowing waves of the covers to distribute the evil odors.

*****

At Kis' week end sitter, Mrs. Olsen's, there was only one child to contend with, Bjarne, her son, who was double Kis' age and size. At eight years of age he was not as messy as Kis when it came to meal times. He got to eat in the kitchen and she had to eat in the laundry porch. She tried hard not to drop a single crumb. One particular day, Mrs. Olson scolded, "Now listen to me! I just got through sweeping this porch and look at the crumbs. It's good enough weather outside, out on the step with you, Kis."

Once outside, she got punished further when she bit into her jam sandwich and hadn't noticed that a bee had landed on it. "Ouch!" Kis cried out then muffled herself, ashamed. She wept without making a sound, waiting for the stinging burn on her tongue to go away.

*****

Mrs. Olsen enjoyed her afternoon naps. Each day, she said the same thing, "You play outside. Dare not disturb me, or have a nap yourself. Bjarne, if you want

12

your allowance this week, you mind Kis, do you hear?" He grumbled but agreed,

"I really don't like playing with a baby. Come on then you annoying little pest. March around the apple tree. Not like that, you weak little girl. Your knees got to move right up to your chest, stupid! Hop on one leg over to the clothesline pole," Bjarne demanded, "drop down and crawl, lift one leg in the air and pretend to pee like a dog on a stump." Bjarne turned his head around making sure that his follower was acting to his satisfaction and staying close, "we are still dogs, stick your nose in the air and sniff. Sniff harder, again."

Kis winced, Bjarne's chubby bum, straining behind the tight brown corduroy knickers, cut the meanest fart ever. Bjarne collapsed with laughter. "Ha! Ha! I got you good."

CHAPTER 4

Bedstemor, Emma and Bedstefar, Aage—Kis' maternal grandparents lived on a farm, not far from town. Snug and secure were the nights when she was allowed to burrow down between them in the big feather bed. Sleeping among them was reserved for stormy nights, after a bad dream, or if she felt unwell. They wore identical long white nightshirts and caps. She giggled at the way they dressed for bed. Kis began making excuses trying to be with them more often.

Wise Bedste said "If you feel too lonely down in the hall chamber we'll make up the chesterfield, here in the day room right next door to us."

Kis clapped her hands and said, "Goody! I won't be scared of the earwigs, then. They wait for you to fall asleep and then they march right into your ears and play the drum." She continued about how often they crawled all over the whole wall and how she stayed awake afraid they would crawl into her ears. Bjarne warned her of them once when they saw the crawlies in a wood pile at his house.

"Why do you think they are named that way?" Bjarne asked. "The creepy crawly earwigs play eardrums. You know nothing, stupid."

On the sofa, Kis drifted into sweet dreams to the rhythm of the great-grandfather clock and the comforting snoring, coming from the room, close by.

During the day she followed behind one or the other. After the midday meal came quiet time. Bedstefar read his paper. The postman, on his bicycle, delivered early morning. Kis wangled her way onto his knee and sat snug in his arms and drifted off for a little nap.

"Ooh! That's prickly. Stop that!" she protested but giggled when Bedstefar gave her a whisker rub to wake her up.

*****

A typical day in haying season started with the usual early morning, oatmeal porridge. "Hurry you little sleepy heads. Get on this wagon before we pull out without you," said Bedstefar.

He, the hired hand, and aunties, Lilly and Asta had been up for hours—milking and feeding the livestock. They were now on the wagon that was hitched to the horses, Musse and Bruno. Bedste boosted Kis and her three girl cousins onto the wagon. The horses strained. Restless, they jerked at the reins making the ride bumpy. While in the field, the girls raked hay until tired. They found mice, frogs, and a myriad of insects, catching, and studying them before release. Proud, statuesque storks pranced around, paused on one leg, and scrutinized the people in the field. All was well. Everyone belonged.

*****

Bruno and Musse moved steadily, rhythmically, slowed by the long hot sunny day and their heavy burden. The cousins dozed in a delicious slumber on the way home. Not fully asleep, but with eyes closed—Kis listened to the hypnotic clip clop of hooves. She recognized their location by the different sounds made by the horses. Ringing hooves meant pavement—the highway. Soft thudding hooves—dirt road, crunching grinding hooves—gravel drive, and distinctive sharp clatters meant they were on the cobblestones in the farm yard.

CHAPTER 5

What is going on in the barn today? She decided to investigate and leave Bedste to manage by herself. Kis felt bored watching the pressing of the tablecloths as they rolled through the huge squeaking mangle. Bedstefar welcomed her as his second shadow most anytime. He even started training Kis for some chores, one of which was herding the milk-cows home to the barn from the pasture. Bedstefar would say—You must pay attention to the closure of the pathways on your way down to the pasture. Take hold of this wood piece like this and walk with it over to this post on the other side. Slide the wire hoop over this post. See how the barb wire is right across the path. You close the next one. Never, ever, forget. These dumb cows might take the wrong turn—She memorized his words.

This time, as she entered the barn, instead of the usual—Hey girl what you up to now?— she heard, "Hey girl best you leave this barn right now! This is no place for a little girl today. Go on back with Bedste! Go on!"

Bedstefar sounded annoyed. She pretended to leave the barn but placed herself to watch without being noticed. The goings on in the barn all started with the arrival of a truck, delivering a pig. At a distance, Kis observed the loud grunting pig being led into a pen with one of the sows. When he started attacking the sow by jumping up on her, she forgot all about how she was not supposed to be there. Frightened, she yelled out, "stop him, please, stop him! He's goanna kill the sow! Make him stop!"

"I thought I told you to get? Now get at once!" Bedstefar yelled back at her.

She ran, sought comfort and Bedste's sympathy, "Don't you worry? The boar will soon be gone. Bedstefar hired him to service the sow and she will have little piglets."

"Why didn't he just get the vet to come with a tube of piglets to squirt into the sow like he does to the cows with a tube of calves? I get to watch and it's yucky when the vet sticks his whole arm into the cows. It comes out with poop all over it. I don't wanna be a vet when I grow up. Bedste, I like the way chickens have babies. Is the boar a man pig? Will he be the dad of the baby piggies when they are born?"

"Yes you might say that."

"I know babies come from their mummy's tummy. Was I squirted into my mum's tummy with a tube?"

"No"

"Where is my daddy, then? I don't have one and other kids do."

"Ask your Mum. Now let's collect eggs."

"I like touching warm eggs."

*****

When grandkids were past napping age, they had to play outside. They made tents out of old blankets, chased and caught kittens, dressed them up in doll clothes and walked them around in a doll pram. On a miserable weather day, the four cousins sat at the kitchen table and looked at books, and colored. Once in a while when they were well behaved they had one of their favorite treats.

"Okay girls, off to the henhouse and pick out your fresh egg. I need the whites for meringue. Today you may make stirred egg yolk," Bedste announced.

Jumping with joy the girls ran to be first. Kis loved sticking her hand under the warm hen. She felt for the biggest egg and hoped it had a double yolk to take back to the kitchen. Bedste, separated the yolk from the white. The girls became busy, quiet, and content. They stirred the yolk until their fingers ached—in competition with each other to whip up the whitest and fluffiest mixture. When the tablespoon or two of sugar was dissolved, the girls savored the concoction. Sometimes, for variety, they added a teaspoon of cocoa powder.

*****

Christmas cookie baking included Bedstemor, aunties, cousins, and Kis. It took two to three days from dawn until late afternoon. The little girls popped cookie dough into their mouths, on the sly. They learned not to complain of sick tummies afterward for it did not deserve sympathy. They planned when they grew up, and had their own homes, they were going to make and eat as much raw bread and cookie dough and cake batter as they desired.

The Christmas of 1953 would forever stay etched into Kis' memory. The one she wanted to re-create for others, with a setting to promote the same warm feelings she was fortunate enough to have experienced.

Bedstefar, Kis and her cousins had been busy all afternoon, tying sheaves of grain—an offering to the birds. They set out saucers of cream for the cats in the barn. Most important, it was their duty to take the old chipped brown and beige striped crockery casserole dish, filled with rice porridge, up into the attic for Santa's elves. The dish was licked clean. *Boy, oh boy, how hungry those little elves are. They must work hard,* Kis thought. Besides working hard in the toy factory, they helped Santa the whole month of December by placing nightly treats in a shoe placed in the window—one shoe, for each child.

*****

Bedstemor's cooking was always delicious but at Christmas it was exceptional. Her dinner table had been decked out in all the best linen and china, while the aroma of the festive traditional foods permeated the air. There was roast goose, crisp and brown, stuffed with sweet apples and prunes, served with hot, sweet and sour red cabbage, rich brown gravy and white boiled potatoes. For dessert there was fluffy lemon mouse with whipped cream.

The food the children looked forward to most of all was the one served first—traditional rice porridge which was served hot, sprinkled with cinnamon and sugar, and a lump of cold hard butter in the middle. Who would find the hidden, peeled almond in the rice porridge? All eyes searched the faces around the table watchful for any sign of almond discovery. Bedstefar pretended to have puffy cheeks and Bedste coughed as if choking on the almond.

The winner revealed it after everyone cleaned up their bowl and then received a special gift, a chocolate Santa, or perhaps a marzipan pig, with a red bow around its neck. After Christmas Eve dinner the children waited patiently for the adults to clear away the food and to do the dishes.

*****

With eyes wide open and butterflies fluttering in full tummies, Kis held tight on to her younger cousins' hands. They giggled in suspense as they waited for the double doors to open to the special-occasion parlor. It was time. They heard movement behind the double doors, and then Bedstefar opened them wide.

There, in all its splendor and glory, towered the fresh cut, magnificent conifer, right in the center of the room. It glowed with real candles, pure white. Underneath the tree branches was a bucket of sand and one of water, just in case of a fire. Most noticeable of all were the pretty wrapped packages. Around the room were overstuffed comfy chairs, upholstered in red crushed velvet. In between, on small tables were crystal dishes filled with a variety of Christmas treats: apples, oranges, nuts, dates, figs, homemade cookies, and marzipan confections.

While the candles, on the tree lit up the room, everyone joined hands and circled the Christmas tree. They sang all the loved hymns and carols. Afterwards, the candles were blown out and the gifts were handed out. In the middle of all this, jolly old Santa showed up bringing another gift for the children who had been good throughout the year.

Kis received a picture book. No words, just pictures. There were two characters in the book, a mother and a girl child performing activities together around the home: washing, ironing, cooking, and cleaning. She loved the mother in her picture book. She had a sweet smile, and in some of the pictures, hugged and kissed her daughter.

Then there was the glimmering Cinderella figurine music box. Her dress was blue with silver sparkles that came off onto her hands. Kis un-wrapped a doll with a porcelain face, hands, and feet, but the body was of cloth stuffed with something poky. The doll came with a bamboo-rail crib. It had embroidered lace bedding in pink floral. Kis hugged and kissed the new doll and named her Dolly Lise. The doll received many more hugs and kisses until the day Kis was forced to abandon her.

*****

The Cinderella music box figurine did not have a happy ending as in the real fairytale. Bedstefar brought Kis home in his little grey Morris car after a weekend visit to the farm.

The apartment was an awful mess. *Maybe the window had been left open and a vicious wind blew through it placing contents in different places than they used to be in.*

"Clean up the mess, Cinderella is not mendable" said Ava.

Kis squeezed the tears to go backwards. She feared her mother's wrath was sure to come her way as it always did when she cried. Her hands were covered in sparkles that once adorned Cinderella's dress. Careful, not to break the pieces further, Kis placed her broken Cinderella in the trash can. *Dolly Lise will be sad tonight when I share the sad, bad news with her and I don't know how it happened.*

CHAPTER 6

Kis was leader and mediator among her three girl cousins, and tolerant of the others considering they were younger. One particular evening, Kis lost her cool, broke into tears and rushed to tell Bedstemor, "I am mad at Bett. Once I saw her use my face cloth and I told her no! Now it is stinky and Bett must have used it on her bum!"

Bedste asked, "Did you see her use it?" Kis shook her head. "How do you know then?"

"Well, just you smell it! It stinks rotten!"

Bedste took a sniff and explained, "My dear, this is not a bum smell. Face cloths can go sour if they are not wrung out."

Kis believed the explanation with surprise and went in search of Bett, "Sorry, please don't cry? I'm sad. I didn't know."

*****

One night lightning struck followed by explosive deafening noise. The girls, even Kis, pulled covers over their heads. They were in the huge bed, just off the fancy parlor, away from the other bedrooms in the farm house. Sisters, Bett and Jilly lay rigid, eyes wide open, staring. Nita cried hysterically, hiding under the feather tic. Kis, with shaky voice said, "Oh now, now, it's nothing. It's happened before and it will go away again. You girls must know it's only Thor up there making a lot of noise about nothing." Kis tried to remember the tale, as Ib once told her.

When she heard footsteps, Kis said "Oh good here comes Bedste.

"Thunder woke me, here I am. You girls might like to keep me company by candle light in the kitchen. We can have warm milk, until the storm is over."

"Oh yes! Are you sca - scared too Bedste?" Nita gulped, swallowed hard and took Bedstemor's hand.

"No! But who in the world can sleep through flashing and rumbling, loud enough to wake the dead?" Bedste grinned and raised an eyebrow.

"Really, Bedste... how will the dead crawl out of their deep holes?" asked Kis.

"Oh, I'm just silly, talking nonsense, teasing you. Of course, they can't get up." Bedste was quick to reply.

Comforting it was, sitting in the dark kitchen at the long table with candle light. Kis was happy. Bedste agreed to serve hot chocolate instead of hot milk. Cows' milk, hot or cold, was a most unpleasant flavor for Kis.

*****

Oranges were rare treats in Denmark, given on special occasions. One appreciated and savored an orange for as long as possible.

Once at a family gathering at Bett's and Jilly's parent's farm, the four little girls were presented with plump, fragrant, juicy oranges. Quite the work of art, peeling back the rind exactly until half the orange was exposed and a sugar cube pushed into the top. Eating an orange was like a contest—be the triumphant, slowest eater, still enjoying when others looked on—wishing they still had theirs left.

Mother Nature called upon three year old Jilly while they slurped their oranges. Where one went, they all went. They were not concerned with propriety or privacy, nor did they experience queasiness at the combination of two opposite body functions—eating and emptying— into the outhouse they all squeezed.

"Ooh ha DΛ!" yelled Jilly. 'Plop!' Jilly's was bumped and her orange flipped from her hand, right into the hole as if it were a target and landed, half sunk, in the ooze below.

"Kis you pushed me I want my orange!" Jilly set to howling at her loss.

"Shush, Jilly, shush I will get it!" Kis stretched her arm into the putrid hole, retrieved the prized orange and rushed to the pump in the laundry shed. She worried that her mom heard Jilly scream, and would accuse her. Kis rinsed, rubbed, and rinsed again the filthy, almost ruined orange. Then on her tippy toes, she sneaked into the kitchen, got a brand new sugar cube. With a wide smile, Kis presented Jilly with a nearly new but paler orange, saving the day.

"Thank you, Kis, and I got another sugar cube. Ha and you guys don't."

Some of Jilly's escapades did not end quite so happy. It happened twice—haystack jumping resulting in Jilly breaking the same arm. The second time was not long after getting her cast off the first time.

24

Bett, Jilly's older sister, was plumper than average. Even amongst the close knit troupe of girls, there was a time when Bett was an object of their entertainment. They had a hilarious time at Bett's expense.

"Fat Sack, Fat Sack, Bett is fat as a grain pack, Fat Sack," the girls taunted.

At first Bett retaliated, mouthing back insults at the girls, "Skinny Sticks, Bony Knees, I don't care if you tease!"

The brave facade faded and Bett's eyes burst with a dam of tears. The girls became silent and mortified that they hurt their Buddy. One by one, they approached Bett. One took her hand, the second, placed an arm around her back, and the third explained to her, that her size didn't matter. They promised never to tease her about that again.

They got a chance to prove their loyalty. At the local swimming hole, three boys taunted and laughed at Bett.

"Fatty, Fatty two by four, we don't like you, don't come here, anymore."

Four girls against three boys—fists, spit, and kicks. Which group received the worst was hard to detect but the girls felt better about themselves as defenders. When Bedste was told the story, they felt even better, because she praised them for sticking up for Bett.

The boys and girls tolerated each other when they happened to meet at the swimming hole, a small creek that wound its way around and near Bedstefar's, fields. Running, jumping, and splashing around in the water was fun. One day the group pulled an old dilapidated row boat from the grassy shore shoving it into the water upside down. The boat served well for jumping off of it making big splashes. Always inventive and ready for a new game or challenge, the kids decided to hold a contest of who could hold their breath the longest under water. 1-2-3, down they all went at the same time. When Kis needed air, she went up, banged her head against something solid. She was trapped, confused, *what, what to do? The boat, I am under the boat!* Going down and outward from her trap she shot out of the water, gasping for air. The group clapped, happy to see her. Kis won the contest.

The four cousins felt like sisters when they were on the farm. Often long stretches went without seeing one another.

Sometimes they felt divided. Bett and Jilly, sisters, and having a mother, a father and two sets of grandparents, formed one side—Kis and Nita the other side. They each had a mother, neither had a father they knew. Kis pondered on such details, and tried to figure out why it was.

She was intrigued with her own circumstance. At a young age, she picked up on whispered conversations between her relatives, when the opportunities arose.

Fate twisted and shifted all family life in different directions for the four cousins, for Nita and Kis, slow and similar, but for Bett and Jilly—unmerciful and quick.

CHAPTER 7

Kis noticed intrusion in her life when her sleeping place changed from the divan she shared with her mother, to alone on two chairs pushed together.

In the morning there was a man on the divan with Ava. "Kis cover your eyes, don't peek," Ava commanded, "shut your eyes, while Erling gets out of bed and gets his trousers on."

Soon there was a wedding ceremony in Ribe Domkirke, the centuries old church from the 700's.

Getting ready for the wedding had been a lot of fun. Ava took Kis to the hairdresser where they were both fussed over and made to look nice. Ava had put setting lotion and wave clamps in her man's hair in the morning. When mother and daughter returned from the beauty salon, he was most eager for Ava to complete his wedding day look. Kis observed Ava with him, laughing, teasing, and touching each other. *Mum is happy today—how pretty she is when she smiles.*

Kis had a new tulle dress, new shoes with straps no orthopedic boots today, and a bow in her hair, big and white. She worried a little about her toothless smile. Kis was most impressed by the little blue velvet, ring box, now hers after the wedding ceremony.

*****

Ava's husband, Erling was tall, pleasant looking, with brown hair. He went to work in the morning and returned in the evening. Every work day, he wore khaki pants and a shirt with a pocket for a wide flat pencil. He smelled of sweat and wood. *I wonder if he is supposed to be my dad but nobody told me. What will I call him? I guess I will call him, you.*

Ava had already threatened Kis one day when she spilled her milk, "don't you forget there is a man in the house now and he will get after you if you misbehave."

"I haven't been bad. Why will he get after me?"

"Don't give me any lip or pouty look. Go get coal from the cellar, be quick about it or the rats will eat you!"

Did he like her? Like Ava, he didn't hug or kiss her. He was for the most part quiet. If he was angry or the least bit disapproving, Kis knew right away. Erling had a look. *He is a stepfather. Maybe I better not like him too much. I have to be careful.*

*****

Once on a picnic out by Ribe Dam, with Nita and her family—the two girls, off by themselves—compared sentiments about their new fathers.

Nita proudly said, "My dad is real nice. We play games and he laughs a lot. He even tucks me into bed and reads me a story."

Kis, downtrodden replied, "I don't like mine. He is kind of scary, and I don't think he likes me. He has a look like I don't know, it just scares me."

"I like your dad, he looks nice." Nita said, "Come, let's jump on their backs and wrestle with them."

"Oh No, I'm not! I will get into trouble," Kirsten protested.

Nita thought a little while, and then she said, "Kis want to trade. I'm not afraid of yours. He won't get mad at me and mine won't get mad at you!"

The two unsuspecting fathers, sitting on the bank of the reservoir, talking man talk, were unprepared. They were bowled over by the exuberant Nita and the hesitant Kis. It was fun! Kis wondered if it would have been fun if they had not traded.

*****

Kis went down to feed the ducks one evening after supper. Out back, of the housing complex, where they lived, there were remains of an old castle, surrounded by a moat where the ducks often swam. There were remnants of an old castle and a beautiful statue of Queen Dagmar standing in a boat, hands shielding her eyes from the sun as she waited for her husband the King, to return.

Kis came here often, sometimes alone, sometimes with play mates, sometimes for games of imagination.

While she fed the ducks her tummy cramped and cramped. She did not want to stop until each duck got a morsel and the bread was all snapped up. She squeezed her buttocks tight. This often happened when she played hide and seek. Then she would get found, rushing out of hiding, hurrying to the toilet.

I just have to make sure each duck gets some and to break up the bread. They can't manage big pieces. Ooh!

Ooh! She squeezed and stood still. Waited, tried to force it to go away—no luck—the urge persisted.

Kis started the trek back but....the need was great. In horror she felt it squishing out. Kis dashed behind a hedge, dropped her drawers. To her disgust, it was soft and messy. There was nothing at all to wipe with except the tall grass nearby which Kis used to the best of her ability. She returned to the apartment a short time later.

"What took you such a long time? Get undressed and hop on to the kitchen counter, it's time for your sponge bath and then off to bed," said Ava.

Kis' baths were still given by her mother. It was too awkward for Kis to do by herself without a shower or a bath tub. After assessing the condition of Kis' private parts, Ava screamed out "You stupid girl! Did you eat grass and get diarrhea? Your underwear will never come clean!" Kis received a spanking. Feeling embarrassed she wondered if Erling saw her bare bum?

The same evening before falling asleep, Kis overheard Erling ask her mother, "Ava don't you think you were too hard on the girl?"

"She needs a firm hand. It's the only thing she understands."

Kis cuddled with Dolly Lise and whispered, "Maybe he likes me a little bit."

*****

When Ava was at work one evening, Kis was alone with Erling. She took a chance, snuck into the tiny kitchen up on the stool and helped herself to a teaspoon of the

30

sugar she loved. 'Ech, spit, spit and gag,' *Oh No it was salt.*

"Kis is everything okay out there?"

"Ya I'm fine, I just need a glass of water. I am really thirsty"

"Do you need help?"

"No please let me do it myself" Kis thought she heard him chuckle. *There must be something funny in the paper.*

*****

Soon the three of them moved to a larger apartment, one with a separate bedroom for the newlyweds. Kis slept alone in the sitting room. The apartment was on the third floor but there was a flush toilet outside in a separate building, however, Kis still used a chamber pot most of the time.

Six months after their wedding, Ava went to the hospital in the middle of the night, to give birth to a strapping healthy baby boy, named Karl. Kis was happy to go stay at the farm.

*****

During this particular stay, Aunt Asta was in a gymnastics competition. Kis was taken along with her grandparents to watch the competition and cheer for Aunt Asta.

There was an interruption—hurry scurry into the little Morris car they went. The mood was silent and sadness floated around in the car on the way to Ribe hospital. Kis knew to be still and quiet.

Bedste explained to her, "There has been an accident. Uncle Kaj was riding his bicycle when he was hit by a car. We haven't got time to take you somewhere to stay, be good, be quiet little Kis, won't you please?"

Kis felt somber, at the same time important, and mature to be included, on an otherwise adult experience. She sat quiet without talking and thought about how children could not visit at the hospital. She had not been able to see her mother or new baby brother yet. *Will I see them tonight?*

Aunt Inger was also in the hospital, she gave birth to a baby brother for cousin Nita. Nita and Kis both got step fathers around the same time. *Will cousins, Jilly and Bett come to the hospital and see their dad lying in his hospital bed? I think they will cry.* Oh boy! Oh boy! This was exciting in the dark of night her thoughts raced.

After arriving at the hospital the trio was greeted by a nurse, "Follow me," she said. "Your son-in-law's condition is grave. Your daughter is by his side."

Aunt Annie was with her husband, waiting for her parent's. The room was dark and quiet, except for Aunt Annie's weeping and whispering between the adults. Uncle Kaj lay in the bed, unrecognizable, with his head completely bandaged. It seemed as though time and activity froze for a long time for Kis. She stood silent, unnoticed, observing the tragic scene in front of her. There was no thought in her head of mothers and babies, just of poor Uncle Kaj and how he must hurt. Kis' throat felt as though it was blocked. The burning brimming tears overflowed, trickling down her cheeks. Uncle Kaj died then.

A nurse pulled the sheet over his face and said, "I am sorry but Kaj is no longer with us."

Now it was Bett and Jilly without a dad, what a nice dad he had been always giggling and teasing his girls, Kis thought.

*****

For a while, visiting the farm was sad. Aunt Annie was always crying which made Bett and Jilly cry too. Bedstemor would always shoo the girls outside whenever the crying got started.

The girls had many conversations about what it might be like to be dead. They all agreed—it must be horrible to be in the cold dark ground. How will the people from the graves come out and go all the way up to heaven, they speculated. Lying on their backs, on the grass, they searched the clouds scudding by—hoping to catch a glimpse of Uncle Kaj up there, with angel wings. Kis and Nita, both optimistic, assured Bett and Jilly, maybe they would get a new daddy just as they had.

That did not happen as the tragedy worsened. Aunt Annie's grief was deep. She died of a broken heart a year later. Kis thought it meant, if you felt bad enough inside, your heart must break, in two, killing you in an instant. Once when visiting Uncle and Auntie's grave and after Bett and Jilly placed flowers, Bett remarked, "We should all help getting a ladder down inside. They can climb back out."

It always seemed as though grown-ups were uncomfortable with the talk about death. They changed the subject.

Kis, for one, became hesitant with questions, about many mysteries of life. She thought she was a bad girl, if she asked.

Mother always replied the same way, "That is not to talk about! Go away and play."
The best way to get knowledgeable was to eavesdrop, and snoop through her mother's personal papers and medical books—that way she avoided her mother's anger.

CHAPTER 8

Erling had a motorcycle with a sidecar. Once, on a nice summer day, he invited Kis to come for a ride, "hop on the back of the motorcycle, I will take you for a ride out to the ocean." They walked along the beach picking up shells and interesting pebbles to take back home. The ocean waves rushed onto the sand. The thundering noise of the water competed with the shrill cries of the seagulls.

"Will you bring me here again?" No answer came. Kis skipped along, zig zagging to miss the waves.

*****

When Christmas time rolled around, Erling suggested, "I think we need more to decorate with, not for the tree, but a scene to sit on the book shelf, under the window there."

The next day, after they shopped together for supplies, Erling and Kis sat together and cut and pasted. Together they created a beautiful winter scene. A cabin emerged from a shoe box with snow on the roof, made of cotton batting. There was a pond which was a round small mirror with little red pipe cleaner elves skating on it. The small house had red tissue paper in the window openings. Erling put a small light bulb inside creating a warm glow.

When gift opening came, Kis loved the doll house Erling made for her as a gift. It had real lights and miniature furniture. She spent many hours fantasizing how happy life must be for the small family inside.

*****

The fair came to town, and Erling took Kis and allowed her to go on any ride she wished. He went to a shooting gallery and kept shooting, on and on until he won a miniature porcelain tea set, which he gave to her. At bedtime she whispered to Dolly Lise, "I know Erling likes me but he doesn't hug me or kiss me like I see other dad's do. I guess only my real Dad would do that if I could find him."

*****

When Karl smiled and gurgled, she was euphoric––a real live doll for her to cuddle and love. Her little brother loved her back.

35

It did not take long before she was trusted and expected to be an active care giver at the age of seven. Now in grade one, she went by her name of Kirsten.

*****

Outside, on a warm spring evening, Kirsten and all the neighborhood children played 'Kick the Can.'

"Kirsten, come now! You have to come in!" Ava's voice, loud and clear, interrupted her fun. *Oh no! What have I done now? Gee whizz! I want to stay out and play.*

"We are going out for a while and we know what a big girl you are now. You can babysit your little brother. The door will be locked from the outside so you can't go out to play and no one gets in except us. Do you hear me?" Kirsten nodded, yes.

"Karl is in bed for the night. You go to bed at nine o'clock, understood?" Ava demanded an affirmative answer. Again, Kirsten nodded.

After her parents left, she felt quite lonely and just a little bit scared. She pulled a chair over to the window which she opened, able to hear and see her playmates still at play outside in the street. Ulla spied her in the window and came running over, "why did you leave? Come on back out, we're still playing. We don't have to go in yet."

"I can't! I'm babysitting," she replied importantly.

"Well then, I'll come in and play with you!"

Kirsten thought a while about how no one should be coming in. Anyway, the door was locked, but it would be nice having someone there with her, "you have to climb in the window and keep it a secret. I will catch big trouble if we are found out."

Ulla was inside in a flash. They chose to dress up as fancy ladies and visit each other for tea. Ulla's apartment was the kitchen and hers was the living room. Both girls dressed privately in each of their pretend homes. When Kirsten was ready to visit, she knocked on the kitchen door.

"I'm not ready yet," chanted Ulla.

Kirsten was getting a little impatient, wondering what was taking so long. She heard Ulla moving about quite a bit, on the other side of the door, "what is taking you such a long time? What are you doing?"

"Oh don't worry! I'm ready now. Come in." The girls had fun with their playacting until Ulla snuck back out the window and Kirsten went to bed.

*****

The next day when she came home from her grade one class at Ribe elementary school she got in the door before her mother's angry voice thundered at her.

"Whatever possessed you to be such a thief? How do you expect to get away with it? Early this morning, I took down my milk money can and found it empty. What a rotten child you are. We trust you and you turn around and steal from us? Well I am telling you, it won't be tolerated." Ava grabbed her and gave her a burning, stinging, wallop across the face, then sent her to bed without supper.

Kirsten tried to say she did not take the money. She was real certain Ulla did because she took a long time. She must have got a chair, reached up to the shelf and emptied the money can. She cried when her mother demanded an apology and she said she was sorry but followed with "I did not take it though." The next day at school, she searched out Ulla and the conversation went back and forth.

"I did not."

"You did." Kirsten's frustration exploded. She grabbed Ulla by her braid, gave it a good yank, and then smacked her face hard, making her nose bleed. The head mistress treated fighting among students as a serious offense. Kirsten was sent home with a note of explanation which was to be returned and signed by a parent. She did not bother trying to explain. *What was the use*? Another thumping and early to bed as per her usual punishment

Ava yelled at her, "You are unmanageable and rotten to the core. I never wanted you in the first place. I should have given you away. You are nothing but work and trouble." Kirsten hated being thought of as a bad girl. *I know I'm not all bad.*

*****

The next Saturday, Kirsten observed a neighbor lady outside hanging up the wash and that gave her the idea to do something nice for her Mum.

"Hi Mrs. Johansen, sure was good cinnamon toast you served to Mum and me the other day you asked us for tea. We will like to come again. Today is a good day to ask us because my Mum needs to have something to be happy about. Do you want me to run and ask her?"

Mrs. Johansen wore a big smile on her face and graciously agreed, "You know I could use a break from my washing. Go on, get your Mum and come for tea."

Wow this is just great! She hurried in to the kitchen. "Mum! Mum! Guess what? We are invited to Mrs. Johansen's. She asked me to invite you right away! Isn't that nice Mum? Won't that make you happy?" Away they went for a nice time. Kirsten felt satisfied that she had done some good.

CHAPTER 9

One day, home from school the little cherub was not there, just Mum and Erica, Karl's sometime baby-sitter. Erica babysat during the days Ava worked. She was crying and saying how she didn't know how she would ever get over this.

"What is it? What happened? Where is my little brother?" cried Kirsten who was beginning to feel scared.

"He had trouble walking in his new boots and tripped on the carpet over at Erica's today. Both his hands got burnt on the coal heater," answered Mum.

Kirsten started to cry. Erica put her arms around her, "I am sorry, it happened fast, it's my entire fault," Erica sobbed.

Ava scolded them both, "Crying doesn't help anything. Stop it."

*****

Karl spent a few days in the hospital. Shortly after he came home Ava and Erling rushed him back in the middle of the night, to calm his painful screams. Kirsten tried blocking her ears not to hear him. Her heart felt like it might break.

As soon as Karl's hands were well mended, Kirsten was happy to take him out on the sidewalk, letting him walk back and forth while she held his walking rein, allowing him independence. He did not want to hold hands.

All was well, until the horse-drawn milk wagon pulled up. Kirsten dropped the rein attached to Karl, ran to the kitchen window and yelled, "Milkman is here," she turned around and watched in horror as the exuberant precious little boy wobbled off the curb. He walked right under the old nag, squealed with delight, and stood on tip toe straining to grab hold of the horse's belly. Kirsten let out a blood curdling scream!

Smack—she received a slap across her face, then "You stupid girl keep quiet or you will startle the horse and Karl will for sure get hurt. I just can't understand how it happened? I thought you could take better care of him than that! You are a stupid bad girl!"

The milkman discovered the situation and saved Karl from under the horse. Kirsten, remorseful, was in tears.

"Stop that stupid crying or you will really get something to cry about," her mother said.

"Oh Dolly Lise I feel sad," Kirsten whispered to her night time companion. "I don't know how come everything I do turns into trouble. I think my Mum hates me. I wish she would hug me and kiss me. I hate her. I hate her!" Kis soaked her dolly with her tears until she fell asleep.

*****

Ulla, the thief of the milk money had long been forgiven. Kirsten admired the slightly older girl who was allowed many more privileges than she. Ulla also had no father. She wore nail polish and always had pocket money for candy.

One day while Kirsten rolled a big ball, back and forth, to Karl, Ulla came strolling along. She was looking for someone to accompany her to the train station, to watch the excitement about to happen there.

"Hey you, the summer kids are pulling in today. It will be fun to go watch all those silly city slickers getting off the train, looking lost and scared! They wear stupid name tags around their necks for all the farmers to find their summer kid!" Kirsten thought Ulla's suggestion sounded like a really fun adventure. She wanted to go.

"But, Ulla, I already know my Mum will say no. How can I go?"

"Easy if we hurry, we will be back before they even know you are gone."

"What about Karl? I am supposed to look after him."

"You are no fun! You know that? All you ever do is play with that little kid! A B-A-B-Y! If you don't want to be my friend anymore I will get somebody else to come. I was even going to buy a soda down at the station and treat you too! If you really want to go, just ask Else," Ulla pointed across the street, "ask her to play with Karl till we get back. I will even give her a couple of cents. Ah Come on! We'll have fun!" Ulla succeeded in tempting Kirsten.

Away they skipped down the street. They watched the shy kids as they stood on the platform, some of them frightened to tears, already homesick. The girls were deeply absorbed in people watching, completely unaware of the time and stayed until the sky began darkening.

Kirsten did not saunter alongside Ulla on the way home. Her adrenalin and the grip of frenzied fear, made her run as fast as she could until she reached her street. *Oh! No! Where is Else and Karl?* Butterflies fluttered away in her stomach along with hunger pains. She missed the evening meal. She slowed down, could barely walk with her weak and shaking knees. *What is about to happen.* Kis inched the door open and peeked inside. The kitchen was empty. She wormed her way in. The door squeaked.

Swish—both parents stormed into her sight—stood as menacing towers about to tumble down over the petrified girl.

"You are really going to regret this you horrible child," Ava screamed as she let loose. One of her familiar head shots connected with Kirsten's ear, and made her head bounce sideways onto the sharp little button on the

42

light switch plate. The pain was excruciating on both sides of her head. Her hearing was rather muffled like an echo and her vision was distorted. She was pulled by her hair, marched to the bedroom and ordered to bed at once, followed by various threats of what else would follow for punishment, and no supper for sure.

Kirsten's punishment was completed when Erling, stern faced and silent entered her bedroom, laid her across his lap, pulled down her pajama bottoms and applied a lengthy and painful succession of hard stinging slaps. Her hysterical uncontrollable crying and the slapping caused her to wet herself which she later tried to hide by hanging her pajama bottoms at the head of her bed, to dry overnight hoping Mum would not find this out—it would most likely mean another spanking.

"Oh dear Dolly Lise, everything is all wrong," she sobbed against the cool porcelain face, "Erling is a mean, mean, step dad. Mum is a mean witch. I know they both hate me. Mum never wanted me. Erling don't want me either. Maybe my real dad will find me and want me and . . ."she fell asleep.

Kirsten later learned when Else's mother called Else in for supper, she acted proud and announced that she was babysitting and asked what should she do with the little boy? After hearing the whole story, Else's mother took Karl home to his surprised parents, just getting up from an afternoon nap.

CHAPTER 10

Before long, another brother came into the world. He was named Kaj, and was tiny, dark haired, and delicate. He was the opposite of Karl. When Ava was in the hospital, she had commented that something was wrong with this baby. At first the doctors denied this. It soon became evident, Ava was right. You could tell by the way he nursed. Kaj stayed tiny and undernourished looking. His breathing was labored. It turned out he was born with a hole in his heart. It was important this baby not be stressed in any way. The plan was to wait until age two, when an operation would be performed to mend his heart.

*****

Kirsten did her share to keep Kaj quiet. He was not to waste his strength by crying. He spent lots of time in a little rocking cradle, built by Erling, designed with a convenient foot rest reachable from his own easy chair. Kirsten discovered by placing large rubber bands over the ends of the cradle doweling, she could pretend she was strumming them like an Angels harp. Kaj listened and smiled at her.

*****

During the short life span of this little brother, both Ava and the baby were often absent. There was a combined effort of home care help and a neighbor lady who babysat Kirsten and Karl while mother and son were in one hospital or another. Kirsten didn't mind going to the neighbor's after school.

There were two boys there, one older and one younger than herself. After a while, she was reluctant to spend any time alone with the oldest one because he always wanted to play doctor. This game seemed acceptable to the younger one who was always begging for his turn to be examined, in the examining room, under the bed.

Ava had begun lecturing, Kirsten, "Beware of boys. Don't play any house or kissing games with them, ever! Do you hear me? You may as well learn, boys are bad, and they will hurt you. Boys only want one thing. Stay away from them."

What is the one thing all boys want? She knew better than to ask. Ava did not approve of questions. If she wanted to say more she would. She was apt to give her familiar answer, "We don't talk about that."

Kirsten soon decided this doctor game did not feel right. She felt ashamed. Always, the older boy instructed the younger one to stand watch and warn him if their mother approached. Kirsten felt trapped under the bed. The boy ran his hands all over her body while he rubbed himself with his hands. She did not find any pleasure in his game and wanted no more part of it. *It's something I will get in trouble for.*

*****

One time, the three of them went outside to play, over at the castle grounds, behind the apartment complex.

45

"Hey let me watch you pee? I don't know how girls pee."

Kirsten thought, no big deal, she had seen her little brothers pee many times. She knew boys and girls peed differently.

"Oh c'mon, please—I'll buy you an ice cream cone." She thought awhile. *He didn't have a sister. It might help him to know there is a difference.*

"Fine, but it has to be a large ice cream cone," she said.

*****

When Ava returned, leaving the sick baby at the hospital in Copenhagen, it was a rare, welcome relief for Kirsten. With her mother at home, she was able to avoid the boys next door and resume a more familiar routine at home. She could not tell Ava about the boys and what the three of them had done. She knew most certain—she would get spanked and lectured about bad boys.

Ava had been home for two days when a message came. Kaj took a turn for the worse. She and Erling made plans to travel to the big city, once again.

Bedstemor and Bedstefar came for a visit the afternoon the message came. Kirsten sat coloring, listening in on their conversation. She heard Ava say, "The children will stay with the neighbor. Kirsten can't miss school. Going with you to the farm is out of the question. You have too much to do, to be able to care for Karl."

With a familiar lump in Kirsten's throat and no matter how hard she tried to hold back, the tears pressed on, spilled over, and dripped onto her coloring book. Bedste noticed right away, came over and put her arm around the distressed girl.

"Now, now, my child, what is making you unhappy? Tell me all about it."

A dam opened up inside Kirsten, "please take me home with you? Don't let me go to the neighbors." She was relieved Bedste convinced Ava to change her mind.

*****

When Kirsten got out of bed, Bedste came to her to tell her little Kaj would be sleeping forever, up in heaven. They received a call soon after they tucked her into bed that night. She learned her mother decided to tidy and dust the front room before going to bed. When she came near little Kaj's picture—sudden, without being touched, it tipped over and toppled off the shelf. Ava, in an instance, felt he died. A few moments later the neighbor came with the message— the hospital called, Kaj had passed.

*****

Ava and Erling returned in a rented car. They brought the dead baby, placed in a tiny little coffin, in the trunk. The funeral was taking place the next day but Kirsten was told kids should not attend funerals. She would have to go to the neighbors. Later, Ava told her Kaj looked just like he was sleeping. She thought that was not bad to see. *Why couldn't I have gone?* Kaj was buried next to Ava's real dad who died long before Kirsten was born.

The spot was reserved for Bedste, but she had a new husband and would be buried beside him one day.

*****

After returning to school, her grade one classmates treated her with kindness. The teacher commented on the death of her little brother in front of the class, saying how sorry they were for her.

Kirsten didn't quite understand all the sympathy. *Why do I feel important? They should feel sorry for Kaj— it was he who was dead.* But, it was kind of nice, when at recess, the other girls came up to her, put their arms around her, and said they were sorry for her. The boys didn't say anything to her which was just as well as it was better to avoid them.

CHAPTER 11

She never played with boys anymore and was not nice to them. She had been having a problem with the shoemaker's son. He chased her, pulled her hair. Kirsten got back at him by teasing him about his tightly curled bright red locks.

One day after school let out, he poked her in the back. She was overcome with furry and wound up with her fist and let him have it, right between the eyes and a few other places. He was so stunned he didn't fight back. Children formed a ring around them and started cheering for the winner. The poor lad ended up crying, laying on the cobblestones with a bloody nose. She turned her back on him and marched home. *He might leave me alone now.* Kirsten decided not to talk about it.

*****

She enjoyed school, but not the hot lunches. The frumpy looking cook always had a cigar in her mouth and smelled of sweat. It made Kirsten's stomach churn. One day she found cigar ash in her cabbage soup.

She much preferred her own heavy dark rye bread sandwiches from home. Rye bread with lard and sugar was better than the slop at school. The kids each received a small glass bottle of ice cold milk each day. Whenever someone was absent, she hoped she was chosen to have an extra.

*****

Kirsten was a good student, adept at learning, and welcomed the praise the teacher gave to her. She made one really good friend, Helga Thun. Helga lived on the same street as her, but on the nice end of it where there were big fancy houses not the end that was a low rent area.

Helga's father owned a grocery store as well as the house they lived in. Somewhere in between Helga's house and hers, lived a girl by the name of Rita, whose mother did not allow her to play with Kirsten. No reason for it

Rita knew of, just a fact, but she was allowed to play with Helga.

When Rita celebrated a birthday party, Kirsten felt sad. She was not invited, but figured out a way to attend the party. She picked flowers from the beds along the way to Rita's house. She climbed the stairs to the front door with butterflies in her stomach. Rita's mother opened the door.

Kirsten curtsied, "Good Day, may I please come to the party?"

At a loss for words, the woman gestured her in, cleared her throat and called out, "Rita you have another guest." She took the flowers to put in a vase.

*****

Helga and Kirsten played various games at Helga's house. They never played at Kirsten's. They didn't want to. Helga's father's library was a place they were not allowed into. Whenever they saw an opportunity, they sneaked in and looked through many different books. There were pictures in books and magazines of naked humans, covered in scars, sores, lacerations, and tattoos. They resembled skeletons covered in skin. There were pictures of dead rotting bodies, all to do with World War II and the Nazis and the Jews.

The girls promised each other "cross my heart, hope to die" not to talk about what they had seen. They knew for certain they would be in a heap of trouble, if found out. They were glad not to have lived then!

Sometimes, the girls played with paper dolls. One day they decided to play doctor. They pretended an ice cream stick was a rectal thermometer. The girls didn't really push it into the anus. They just placed it in the crack of the bum cheeks.

Mrs. Thun opened the door, saw and then said, "All right girls, it's much too nice to play indoors today, out in the yard you go! Please! Do not play this game anymore. You might hurt each other with that stick. Promise me?" Outside they went.

"Helga, your Mum is really nice. If it was my Mum, we would have been spanked hard," Kirsten confided in her friend.

Helga's entire family, including her dad and her two brothers were nice and always happy, thought Kirsten. She liked being with them, watching television, and eating tomato sandwiches. She ate her first tomato sandwich with salt and pepper. At home she ate sugar on it.

CHAPTER 12

Ava worked at the mental institution in Ribe. There were old people hugging dolls and drooling, hanging around the chain link fence, babbling at anyone going by. Inside in an auditorium, retarded children were tied into strait jackets, fastened to the climbing apparatus along the walls.

Kirsten was made to go there for weekly baths. One time, Ava hugged her in front of two Mongoloid boys. *Why is she hugging me and laughing?* Kirsten squirmed.

The two children stormed and pulled at her. Ava let go of Kirsten and hugged the boys instead saying, "See how much they love me?"

There was an assembly of retarded children in the bathing and toilet areas at the same time Kirsten went for her bath. The toilets had no doors. She objected to using the toilet in full view of the others and often gagged at the smells in the area.

"Don't be uppity, what do they know or care? One bum is the same as another," Ava said as she tugged Kirsten's clothes off.

CHAPTER 13

Kirsten eavesdropped as she loved to do and heard, "We are finished with this small time, stuck in the mud, going nowhere, Ribe. Let's move to Copenhagen!"

"Yes, I think it's an excellent idea. Everybody knows everyone's business here. I am tired of my interfering relatives.

*****

Bedste gave Kirsten sympathy on the last visit before their move. The two of them got together for a little huddle. "Oh Bedste, my heart is breaking. I am sad. I might even die of a broken heart."

"I feel bad too. We will all miss you. Try to think about something good coming out of this. In the summer, you can be our little city slicker, and come on the train for vacation. I will visit you in the big city. My sister lives in Copenhagen. I will write her a letter and ask her to take you to her house, sometime. You will get to know her two daughters. Do you remember Willy, that nice man, the sailor who visited all of us last year? You know—he gave you a big weather balloon he brought with him from his navy ship. He is in Copenhagen when he's not out to sea. You will learn to be a fancy young lady, speaking with a Copenhagen dialect."

"I don't want to talk like someone from Copenhagen, and get teased when I come here. I bet I will get teased when I go there. I will never find new friends. They won't like me, I know it."

*****

Kirsten resigned herself to the move. She was silent all the way and answered only when spoken to. Erling bought her a chocolate bar and a comic book to enjoy on the long train ride to Copenhagen. She kept staring at the comic, but never turned a page. *Will Helga write? How was their salty black licorice drink going to turn out?*—The girls loved the strong licorice they could buy at the candy store. They thought a licorice drink would be delicious and they put three sticks of licorice in a soda bottle of water, but the black stuff did not dissolve before Kirsten had to leave. *Maybe I'll make licorice water in Copenhagen all by myself.*

53

*****

What a lot of big buildings. Their new home was in a tall building with many stairs heading all the way to the fourth floor. Kirsten wrinkled up her nose at the mixture of odors permeating the air. Each level seemed to have a different smell. *What will our level smell like? This place is dark and ugly! No grass, flowers or trees, just cement.*

Inspection inside the flat was favorable and somewhat exciting. There was more space than any other place they had lived.

"Wow! A real bathroom! Come, look here! May I bathe myself right now? Look at the shower—exactly like a telephone. Oh please let me try it tonight!" She did not stand still for long. Like a streak of lightning she went in and out of each room.

"Perfect, look here, an ice box. Our milk will get really cold just the way I love it. Where do we buy ice?"

The bedroom—only one—was quite big, lots of room for the double bed, the wardrobe, and a brand new set of bunk beds. Kirsten looked forward to sleeping on the top. The walls were a pretty pastel blue, much nicer than the plain wood look, she thought. The front room would be real nice with a plush Ax-minster rug on the floor, cream color with green leaves. In one corner, would sit a brand new dining set that opened up to a big table, for company.

Inquisitive Kirsten surveyed the street scene from the front room window. A feeling of excitement and acceptance crept into her being—a sense of adventure about what lay ahead—just like when the teacher stopped reading out loud—saving the continuance of the story for the next day.

When they first arrived, they used the front stairs from the street. There was a second staircase, out the back of the building, from the kitchen. This led directly to the concrete yard. At the back there was a row of banged up stinky garbage cans. From there, stretched a row of storage cubicles, dividing the yard. Behind the storage area stood a couple of bicycle sheds, one in each corner, and a huge chestnut tree in the middle. There was one swing. Kirsten wondered if many kids lived here. *Only one swing-- probably not.* Directly next, was a wire mesh fence. Through the fence was a beautiful garden with walking path, lawn, and flower beds. *Oh this is nice I didn't know there was a pretty spot here.* The garden was situated in front of a newer section of the entire complex. *If only, we were going to live in one of those suites, with a balcony, facing into the garden.*

The new section had four entries and staircases both front and back. There was an attached portal between the old and new section—from the front street to the back yard. There were big huge doors and they closed at either end, and when shut it was a dark tunnel. In the old section there was as many entries and staircases as in the new section. From the corner of the street, it turned and spread both ways with two more entries and staircases both front and back. The entire complex formed the letter L—a total of twenty entries and staircases, all to the fourth floor. Kirsten counted up the flats—a mathematical chore— seventy six. At age eight she wondered how Ava and

Erling would ever manage to wash all the stairs, sweep the pavement, and handle repair requests and complaints from all the different suites and many people. As caretakers of the complex, their family had to be well informed of the rules of the place and, there were many, Kirsten learned.

Bicycles, toys, or any other item or debris must not be left—even temporarily—on any of the grounds—inside the compound or out on the surrounding sidewalk. Most important of all rules was at least one person in a family was blind—a condition, for the right to live there. This was an institute for the blind. The only exception was the caretakers' family.

Her biggest disappointment was the formal garden was off limits to children. They had to play on the cement. The residents were to be considered with utmost respect, courtesy, and with offers of assistance if necessary. If you met them on the sidewalk, you had to step aside, if their dog was with them, never—no never—distract it, by petting or talking to the working dog. Just let them pass, act polite and identify yourself.

*****

The first few nights in Copenhagen the family spent at Moster's apartment, until their belongings arrived. Moster was her name—never auntie Astrid—she was Bedstemor's sister and even she called her Moster. Kirsten and Karl stayed on with her for one day without Ava and Erling while they settled in. Upon their return in the evening they announce they could move into an apartment with two bedrooms, as soon as one became available.

CHAPTER 14

Kirsten looked forward to moving to the bigger flat. She hated sleeping in the same room as her parents. There were strange noises and conversations in the night. Sometimes she lay silent, straining, waiting for silence before she dare get up to the toilet. Among whispered words, she heard Ava saying, "Hurry up, get it over with" or "Don't do that" or just "No."

Erling groaned and breathed heavily. She wondered if Erling was doing or taking 'THE ONE THING' Mum was always going on about. For certain, she was not about to ask because she knew it was one of those things not to talk about.

*****

When the family did move into a two bedroom, top floor unit, Kirsten did not mind sharing a bedroom with her little brother, and his noises. Nor did she mind the large bedroom served as their everyday dining room. It was nice to have the table and chairs in her bedroom—a place for games, coloring, and her homework. From the bedroom window, she could observe the comings and goings in the courtyard below.

*****

The population at the complex did not include many children and their ages varied. There were about a half dozen of Kirsten's age, an even mixture of boys and girls.

Her first crush was on a young man by the name of Tom. No one knew how much she admired him. He was at least four or five years older than her. He lived on the second floor with his blind parents, and his Bedstemor.

On New Year's Eve, Kirsten and Karl were going down to Tom's for the early evening. Tom's Bedste baked aebleskiver and there was a contest to see how many one could eat. Kirsten ate twenty five of the pancake balls.

Tom sang and played the guitar. *What a fun night!*

"Thank you for having us. It was a really nice New Year's Eve, for us," she said as Tom and his Bedste helped the two children upstairs to bed later in the evening.

Tom and Kirsten hid squeaky toys in Ava and Erling's bed for a New Year's joke.

"Now remember to come downstairs for help if there is any kind of a problem with Karl not sleeping," she was told by the kind woman. Karl slept. Kirsten did not. She upchucked a few times after the many aebleskiver. *Thank goodness no one is at home to find out what a pig I made of myself and for sure I'm not telling, especially not Tom.*

*****

There were a couple of other boys, closer to her own age, living at the complex but she did not care to spend any time with them. They behaved in a creepy, taunting way toward her, after the day she refused to play their game.

The boys had Karen and another of the girls tied by their hands to the post of the bicycle shed. The boys then reached up under the girls' skirts, pulled their panties down, and asked the girls to step out of them. Then, the boys lay on the ground, peeked up at the private parts of the girls. They even tickled them there, with a feather. The girls agreed to go along with this. They didn't seem to mind, but Kirsten hung back, and sat on the swing, watching, instead of taking part.

The boys grew bored with the consenting girls and began to challenge her in a threatening manner. She felt scared by the two pushy adolescents and tried to avoid them as best she could.

Kirsten had been involved in a house playing game in the shed before—a simple game about a regular family. She played the oldest sister—an easy part for her. The boy and girl who played the parent's part spent a lot of time kissing and hugging each other. It was a warm evening and a lot of windows were open all over the complex. Soon, Ava yelled out her window for her to get upstairs now.

"How many times must I tell you not to play kissing games? You know you will receive much punishment if you do. Boys are bad, bad, bad. They only want one thing."

"But Mum…I did not kiss anybody," she defended.

After, whenever the kids in the courtyard started on kissing games, of any kind, she excused herself and left. She did not want any part of her mother's wrath—she was starting to get a little scared of boys and 'the one thing' even though 'the one thing' remained a mystery.

Late one afternoon, after she returned from errands, the two boys were on the stoop at the back entry. One of them stuck out an arm and a leg, preventing her from entering the stairway, "the pass word is a kiss—a kiss from Kis. What's the matter Kis? Are you scared of a little kiss, Kis?"

Somehow she managed to boldly say "My name is Kirsten not Kis and I am not scared of you. I just don't like you well enough, to kiss you, get out of my way. I have to get home before my Mum comes looking for me. When she does, you will be in big trouble."

It worked momentarily—enough time for her to get in and on the first stair. Then, the boys, in hot pursuit, went after her. Her adrenalin raced, she flew, two stairs at a time, heart pounding, breath gasping, and the boy behind her threatening,

"I will get you. Look out for what I will do to you."

"Mum, Mum, I am home," She started to yell from the third landing. She reached the fourth landing and the door flew open.

"What in the world are you shouting for?" demanded Ava.

She stopped short and shrugged her shoulders, too afraid to tell of the boys chasing her.

*****

The girls, of the same age group, in the neighborhood, formed a club. This club was named by

60

taking the first letter from a few bad words the girls knew and putting them together. Their meeting place was under one of the stairwells in the complex—not one where any of them lived—this was to be top secret. The girls practiced saying all the worst words they knew—words not allowed in everyday language. The girls shared what they knew or what they guessed was 'the one thing' and "The Bloody Thing." They were on the right track but not as sure as they pretended to be.

Kirsten's knowledge of the bloody thing came the day she entered the kitchen and witnessed her mother washing bloody rags in a pail.

"What happened? Who is hurt?" She was concerned.

"Never mind, don't worry . . . Someday it will happen, to you too . . . It's a woman thing," Ava, sharp of tongue, dismissed any further explanation or questions.

*****

In the complex lived a girl, Marne. She was in her later teen years and was whispered and giggled about. Kirsten once saw her sitting on the step out back, with legs spread and skirt pulled up. It was a gossipy event because Marne did not have any undies on. There was a young soldier, in uniform, in the audience that evening.

A few nights later, Kirsten and Karen walked into the portal. In the shadows, partly concealed in the corner behind the open door, came groaning and heavy breathing, much like Kirsten heard coming from her parent's bedroom. The difference was Marne was not protesting.

She sounded excited, as did the young man. Kirsten wondered if 'the one thing' was not always bad. The young couple broke apart. He fumbled with the front of his pants. Marne let her skirt drop down. The soldier gave the young girls money, told them to buy ice cream and not to hurry back.

*****

Kirsten missed the dear, comforting, and accepting relatives in Ribe. Often, she reversed her thoughts back to them with great longing in her heart after Ava complained, as if she was to blame for Erling's drinking. *Did Erling drink because he did not want to come home*? She spent many nights hating—one or the other—or both, as she listened to their violent attacks on each other. She had tendency to mostly blame the wicked stepfather. Step parents were the villains in all of the fairy tales and she was convinced her real father would not behave in such a way, if only….

*****

One of her friends at school was giving away some fish—Guppies and Zebra species, if she wanted them.

"Please, may I have an aquarium? I can help to pay for it with my own money."

Her parents looked at one another, "We will talk about it and let you know what we decide. But, you have to keep it clean and remember to feed the fish if our answer is yes."

They didn't say no. Please, please GOD. I promise to be real good.

The next day at school, her friend gave Kirsten good news. She had a small aquarium to give away since her parents bought her a big fancy one. She ran home from school with the news

"Mum, oh Mum, my friend will give me a small starter aquarium for free.

"Well then, I guess you may have those fish to go with the aquarium."

*****

The guppies multiplied quickly. Kirsten learned a pregnant guppy must be separated to give birth, and then quickly take her away from the new born to protect the young from being devoured by their own mother. *Baby guppies cannot trust their mothers either. Why do mothers want to hurt you? I swear, cross my heart, and hope to die. I will love and protect my children someday.* The Zebra fish often jumped right out of the tank. One died. *I have to remember to put a lid on. I don't want to lose more fish.*

CHAPTER 15

Kirsten accepted Copenhagen. She thought the street cars were exciting, running down the middle of the main streets on metal tracks, bells ringing.

Her school was bigger and better than in Ribe. She loved the gym uniform. The girlfriends at school were neat. At recess they paired off in two's. Then, they marched arm in arm around the huge bent and knurled chestnut tree which dominated the whole courtyard.

*****

She became best friends with a girl who lived across the street, kitty corner from her, by the name of Hanne. Her father owned and operated a grocery store on the main floor of their building. Their family lived on the second floor of the same building.

Whenever Kirsten visited at Hanne's, the two girls always played grocery store clerk. At the back end of the apartment hallway was a large closet. On the shelves was an assortment of empty cartons and tins, from items sold in a grocery store. There was play money, paper bags for packing, and pencil and paper for recording accounts of each pretend customer.

*****

In real life, her mother bought all dry goods at Hanne's father's grocery store. Meat was purchased one block down, on the next corner. Fish, however, was bought from a small shop three blocks away on the main thoroughfare. Here, the shops followed one after the other. There was a florist, a ladies clothing store, a delicatessen, a bank, and a hair salon where Kirsten was invited to be a practice model.

Once each week, something different was done to her hair by an apprentice at no cost—only one thing—you let the apprentice do whatever she wanted. She never grew long hair. Mostly she got finger waves but, oh how greasy her hair got in a week! She hated her greasy hair but she was not allowed more frequent washing

"No one gets hair washed more than once a week," her mother told her.

*****

Further down the main drag at the sports center, Kirsten took swimming lessons in the huge, indoor pool. She did not like it. It did not come easy, as the dance lessons she loved taking in Ribe. But, there was something to look forward to on the way home from swimming. After each weekly lesson she was allowed to buy a hot dog for her supper, from the street vendor. *In the whole wide world, there are no hot dogs as delicious as right here— soft, warm, steamed bun, and a bright red wiener with mustard and ketchup.* She decided to endure swimming lessons, until the horrendous day she was enrolled in a competition, with an audience present. Erling came to watch her swim. Kirsten came in last by a length and a half, after the second last swimmer.

"My stomach feels sick. Swimming always gets my stomach feeling sick, and the cold water makes my head hurt too. I think I have to quit swimming." All of these excuses burst out of her mouth when she stood in front of Erling, after the competition. Kirsten fought for control of the cursed tears insistent on flooding her eyesight.

"You know, someone has to be last. You are one of the newest kids to join. Forget about it. It's not the end of the world."

"Sure a good thing Mum's not here. She would be mad and would have told me I didn't try hard enough."

When they returned home Ava's comment to Kirsten was, "Well you should take after me and do better. I was good at sports and earned a bronze and silver in track and field achievements in 1947, a Denmark wide competition. I will show you my brooch of honor. "

*****

Report card time was different. Kirsten was proud bringing them home always with high marks. The comments written by the teacher were good too—She is well behaved, courteous, friendly, and helpful to staff and students alike.

"Make sure you keep it up," her mother commented.

CHAPTER 16

Ava informed her about a blind lady living alone who was looking for someone to do errands for her, "you go see her. She will pay you for running her errands. You can make your own money for some of your necessities. We need all the help we can get around here to make ends meet."

Kirsten liked the old lady right off—if only her apartment didn't smell bad she thought as she tried not to breathe through her nose whenever she was there. The old lady often asked her if she was bothered with an adenoid problem. Kirsten answered, "I had my adenoids out when we lived in Ribe. My Bedstemor and Bedstefar drove me

66

to Esbjerg in their little bus—not a real bus—a Morris car. I call it their little bus. Anyway, it was most awful you know. A nurse held me, wrapped her arms and legs around mine, tight, and it hurt. Then another nurse put a mask over my face with stinky stuff called ether. The next thing I remember—I woke up in the back seat of the car, feeling sick to my stomach and a burning pain up in my nose. If I still sound funny—maybe they didn't do it right."

One day the old lady wanted to know what Kirsten looked like. She stood in front of her and allowed her to feel her face with both hands.

"You are a nice looking young lady," said the blind woman. Kirsten wondered how it worked for blind people and was grateful to be able to see.

*****

The errands took her to the deli and to the library for the blind. She exchanged books and double reel tapes. She stopped on her way back, closed her eyes, and fingered the little bumps to see if she could distinguish any words, no such luck.

The lady paid her one Krone per errand and she did two a week, a real fortune Kirsten thought. Her first pay she went to the florist to buy tulips. *That will sure get Mum to love me.*

"Thank you, that is nice of you Kirsten," said her Mum.

Kirsten smiled with satisfaction. Then Ava instructed her that the money was to be put in a piggy bank. When it was full, it would be taken to the big bank and saved. When Kirsten wanted something, she could pay for it herself if her Mum approved.

She went along with this for a while until her, and her friend, Karen, wanted to go to the bakery to buy a treat. Kirsten took a bread and butter knife, tried to slither out some coins, from her own piggy bank which wasn't a pig but looked like a book. To her horror, the bank did not return to its original shape. She propped it up, on the shelf, the bent side at the back. Away the girls went to the bakery.

CHAPTER 17

Bedste's sister, Moster, came to visit and asked how the children were settling in, after the big move. Ava praised Kirsten, first, the good report card—second, about her savings from doing errands. Ava picked up the damaged bank, and handed it to Moster, "Just feel, how rich the girl is getting."

Coins tinkled out, landed on the floor. Kirsten's face flamed as she expected the worst. Ava's face, also flushed, her eyes narrowed, and she burst out in outrage, "you are a brat! You are a thief! Here I am singing your praises to Moster! What a fool you have made of me!" Ava grabbed hold of her and shook her hard, slapped her hard across the face, and banished her to bed.

Above her own weeping, Kirsten heard Moster say, "Ava, it's her money. She didn't steal from someone else.

Maybe you should consider letting her spend half of what she makes?"

"I will raise my daughter the way I see fit. Thank you much."

It was not the only time Moster interfered with how Ava treated Kirsten.

*****

She spent weekend visits at Moster's, once in a while, and she was a lot like Bedste. Kirsten felt special at her house too. Sometimes they went to the circus, a live play in a theater, and even a taping of a television show for children. Other times they stayed home doing finger nails, talked with the budgie bird that seemed quite human, and visited with Moster's grown up daughters. Once during an outing, Kirsten complained of sore feet.

"How come, a young girl like you has sore feet?" asked Moster.

"Promise not to tell my Mum? My good shoes are too small. They pinch my toes. She will be angry when she finds out—there is no money for shoes."

"She will not be angry, over that. You must be mistaken."

"Don't you know my Mum is mad most all the time, about everything, especially at me? I try hard to please her but it usually goes wrong."

*****

A Short time after, she overheard Moster talking in a low voice to Erling.

69

"Erling you should speak to Ava about her ways, where Kirsten is concerned. I don't think it's right."

"Ya . . . I agree . . . I don't understand my wife. She is touchy, uptight, and flies off the handle without much reason. She claims her nerves are bad."

Kirsten wondered what bad nerves meant. It was not the first time she overheard about nerves, just a few weeks ago.

*****

After, she and her little brother were sent to bed, there was a major fight in the front room between Erling and Ava. It was about another baby—not the right time— an abortion. *What was abortion?* The quarrel got louder and nastier, with much name calling, and then sounds of physical fighting.

Kirsten covered her ears, trembled all over until she screamed, many times over, "STOP IT. STOP IT."

The door to the bedroom flew open and Ava ran in yelling, "See what he has done? He hurt me! He bent my finger so hard! He nearly broke it! Do you see? I am telling you the truth—men are all bad. Mind what I say."

Erling followed her into the children's bedroom, "Settle down, don't involve Kirsten,"

Erling grabbed Ava, roughly. She squirmed, scratched, and kicked. They struggled and banged their way out of the room.

After, she wept . . . and wept. Dolly Lise got soaking wet again. Fantasies about her real father played in her affection starved heart and mind. *How wonderful, if only....*

Her Mum went away for a few days—an abortion. Kirsten learned this by eavesdropping, and realized abortion meant getting rid of a baby. She vowed she would never do that.

*****

Erling and Ava fought often and Kirsten heard more than she wanted to know. Ava was unhappy with all the stairways to clean and complained about all the work she had to do. She did not hesitate to talk about it to Kirsten.

"If he can spend money on drink then I can spend money on the wash. I am overworked, underpaid, and not appreciated for anything I do! I am not spending my day in the loft doing laundry," Ava shrieked in a loud voice, at Kirsten, as if she were somehow responsible, "go on take the clothes to the Laundromat."

She was sent to the coin laundry with a little wagon and didn't mind. It was fun watching the suds and clothes go round and round. The employee at the laundry helped her with the heavy sheets and asked curious questions,

"Why is a young person like you doing the family laundry? Where is your mum?" She felt protective of her Mum in front of this stranger and answered,

"It's hard for my Mum. She has bad nerves and too much other work to do! I'm big enough and important help for my Mum, and I'm nine years old." Kirsten answered in a huffy manner, knowing that further explanation was not to talk about.

*****

With Easter approaching Kirsten remembered the time in Ribe she spent with relatives, who always decorated for the occasion. She visited at her friend, Karen's house and observed the excitement and preparations in that home. Karen told tales of special this and that. When Kirsten got home she approached her mother,

"Mum, you should see how Karen's mother is decorating and planning for Easter. They have it real special there, and Karen told me how wonderful their Easter was last year. Her mother must be a happy and nice lady....Don't you think?"

"Humph!" was all she heard about the subject.

On Easter morning it was a great surprise that Ava set the table with linen and Easter decorations. Kirsten ran to get her decorations she made at school. She was excited and exclaimed,

"Oh Mum!—This is nice! Thank you! Oh I thank you!"

"I had to, didn't I?" Ava's cool reply froze the happiness in midair for Kirsten, making her insides churn once again.

*****

With cold tension in the household, Kirsten felt nervous all the time. Erling came home drunk most nights. There was lots of yelling after the children's bedtime. She never dared to yell out again, no matter how bad it got. She did not want another scene in the bedroom. Mostly she heard about money being in short supply. Suppers were of oatmeal porridge or dry cereal. Meat was a rarity. She felt cheated of her milk quota. She missed it the most, and was allowed only one glass a day. Sometimes she snuck more––hoped not to be caught.

One afternoon, Kirsten was sent outside with Karl, in the stroller.

"Go to the grocer, across the way, buy an orange, and feed it to Karl, in sections, Ava instructed.

"Only one orange?" asked Kirsten.

"There is only money for one. He is small and has a lot of growing to do. Karl needs more vitamins than you, already half grown," Ava replied sharply.

Try as she might, Kirsten was unable to avoid temptation. She ate as much as Karl did, of the juicy orange. It remained a secret. Karl was too young to notice and tattle.

*****

Her clothes were made over clothes. A neighbor lady sewed them from materials which were once Ava's clothes. Kirsten thought they were beautiful. Her most adored was the grey wool coat with a collar of black velvet and a belt with a huge metal buckle. The girls at school admired her coat and made her feel special.

She was happy at school with friends and teachers and she looked forward to extra activities offered. She joined the movie club—once a week a different movie—four weeks in a row. A special field trip to the zoo was a major happening. The children had to pack lunch, but were

73

asked to bring money for a soft drink and a souvenir. Kirsten was allowed to take money from her bank—Ava gave her the key, and permission written on a note for buying Coca Cola, her first taste of the much talked about new pop which could not be purchased without parental consent.

Kirsten bought but not for herself. She looked for something special, with her Mum in mind and chose a shiny porcelain elephant. It looked as beautiful as if it were real, Royal Copenhagen porcelain.

Part of the day was a bit frightening for her when the class stopped in front of the hippopotamus enclosure. She stood in awe watching the huge creature open his mouth wide. She tried to count the teeth in the great cavern. Alas, when she turned around to inform her chums and her teacher, of the number, she discovered them gone. Kirsten could not see them anywhere. She wandered about for nearly a half hour when, to her great joy, she spied her class, lined up for the count before getting on the bus. It was a great relief. She was quick to jump in line, as if she was never lost.

"Thank you, Kirsten. I like the elephant," said Ava.

Kirsten waited with expectation—*Mum must not like to hug or kiss me, and Erling never does either. Mum hugs and kisses little Karl but he is cute.* She hugged and kissed him too. *I wonder if she hugged me when I was a baby.*

CHAPTER 18

It was a happy time when Bedstemor came for a visit to help out, as it was a bad time for Ava, after a miscarriage of a baby, but not an abortion, this time. She arrived late at night and Kirsten was warned by Mum, "Get to sleep girl. Greeting your Bedste will have to wait until morning."

She was so excited—no way, could she sleep, but she did not dare act awake. She was not going to have Mum mad at this time, no way! Nothing must spoil the next two weeks. She pretended to be asleep, but eavesdropped.

"I have been traveling the last little way with pearls in my panties. The clasp broke and now here they are," Bedste said as she undressed herself and talked to Ava then started to giggle as she said, "I hope Kirsten is really asleep. I don't want her going around saying her Bedstemor pearls in her panties."

Near to bursting with laughter, Kirsten held it in. Mum soon left the room. Bedste was to sleep in the bottom bunk. Karl was put to sleep on the floor.

"Hi Bedste, I'm happy to see you! Don't tell Mum I was awake, please," she whispered. Arms reached upward to the top bunk. They hugged one another tight and kissed. The next day, Bedste gave Kirsten a little baby doll, no bigger than Bedste's hand. It looked real and came with lots of doll accessories.

*****

It was a delightful time. Even Ava was quiet, content, and relaxed. One evening, Erling babysat while Bedste, Mum, and Kirsten went out window shopping. One of the store windows displayed a beautiful black satin robe, embroidered with lively colors, oriental style.

"If only Erling could afford to buy me one but, it will never happen in a million years," Ava's voice whined. The next day, Bedste went out by herself and returned with the robe, for Ava.

*****

Kirsten held Bedste tight, "I was happy while you were here. I wish you could stay."

"Now sweetie girl, it wouldn't be fair to Bedstefar. Soon it will be your summer vacation from school and you will come on the summer train with all the other students. Chin up and be a good girl. The time will go fast."

CHAPTER 19

She was so happy! Not one tear spilled over. Kids all around her were nervous, apprehensive, waiting with big fluttering butterflies in their stomachs—waiting to see who would claim them. Kirsten was admired by most of the children for her worldly knowledge of the trip across Denmark. Furthermore, she knew exactly the routine of luggage and name tag matching—It was easy for her. The name tag around a child's neck had to match the name on the letter in the farmer's hand.

A most wonderful thing, in a long time, was about to happen—her, going home, to Bedstemor and Bedstefar, also to her aunts, uncles, and cousins, for the whole two months of summer, as their 'summer kid' from the big city.

*****

Kirsten felt it was different—too different—as though she did not belong anymore. She wished she still lived in Ribe—her town—her home.

The relatives teased her about her Copenhagen dialect and about the fancy airs she must have by now. She was disappointed to be thought of as different.

I don't belong here anymore . . . will I ever feel like I belong in Copenhagen?

"The kids there tease me about my country bumpkin dialect," she confided to Bedste.

"Oh Hon, you will be all right once you grow up a little more, don't worry."

*****

An annual highlight of the summer was Ribe's Tulip Fest and Fair. For Bedstefar and the hired hand it meant extra work—the cows, going to competition were scrubbed and groomed.

Bedstefar's livestock had a reputation of having a high standard. There were many ribbons of honor, from the past, displayed in the tack room. The day before the fair when almost all cows were ready, Kirsten went along to the pasture, to collect the last cow.

"Girl, you take this here lead rope. Hang on to this creature, while I go pump water, for the rest of the critters. Whatever you do— don't you let go!—she can be an ornery one!"

Kirsten felt clammy and weak in the knees, but she did not utter one word of protest to Bedstefar. She stood glued to her spot, on the gravel road, wishing for the time to speed by and for his return.

With only a couple of feet between her and the monstrous, black and white cow, she studied the huge brown eyes, mesmerized in fear, and hardly dared to breathe.

With a great jerk—the miserable cow took off. *I have to make Bedstefar proud.* She did not let go of the rope. Off her feet, dragged along, scraped over gravel, slid through cow paddies, and then finally in the muddy ditch––all of this, she survived without being stepped on, by the cantankerous beast.

"Let go! Let go!" She heard and saw Bedstefar hobbling along with his cane at his top speed. Upon reaching her, he asked, concerned, "Kirsten, my girl, is you hurt? Why are you still hanging on to the rope?" He shook his head and fussed around, and helped her to her feet, then surveyed her condition. Aside from a bit of a road rash, she was physically fine. She was confused. Out of respect of one's elder, she did not say what was racing around in her head.

He told me not to let go. He asks me why I did not. Why I am not praised for hanging on? The dumb cow might be long gone, if not for me? Her good manners won out over the urge to yell it out.

*****.

During the evening, after bathing, hair curling, and much discussion about the many fun things to look forward to the next day, Bedstefar announced Kirsten should lead her beast around the ring at show time, "now since my granddaughter showed the cow her bravery, it will behave better, the next time she takes the lead rope."

She felt choking fear again and stared at him, in disbelief, and muttered, "I don't think she likes me. I think somebody else better walk her round the ring. She might not win anything with me leading her."

"Nonsense, pure nonsense, I will feel proud to have my granddaughter from Copenhagen parading one of my cows around."

*****

The next morning, not a cloud in the sky, brought promise of a perfect day ahead. Kirsten was exhausted from nightmares and worries about the walk-about, in the ring, with the despicable monster. She dared not admit her fear. *The livestock showing and judging takes place early morning. Let it hurry up and be over with.*

*****

Oh! Oh! Now it's my turn! She felt frozen like a statue, hands on hips, unblinking eyes, and staring straight ahead. The hired man approached with stretched out hand, and offered the lead rope to her. Nary a word escaped her lips. Her head moved from side to side in slow motion. He said nothing . . . she said nothing . . . He did an about turn and proceeded into the ring. The announcer began with an introduction naming Kirsten as the leader, but stopped short and said, "I see there has been a slight change in plans," and carried on with his commentary.

Her face colored, and she lowered her eyes in shame. Bedstefar did not comment on her fainthearted behavior. Out of nine of his cows at the show, all placed first in their category, except the monster got a second place ribbon—*Serves her right.*

*****

The rides on the midway, the cotton candy, all helped to put the cow fiasco out of her mind. Best of all were the circus acts in the late afternoon. One of the trapeze artists was a cousin of sorts through, Moster's ex-husband. *She is beautiful with dark hair and eyes.* Bedste commented indeed she looked like a true gypsy. For Kirsten it was special to get to meet her after her performance.

*****

The next day, after the fair, the local newspaper printed an article about the fair activities. There were some pictures, including on of Kirsten, hands on hips, standing right beside Bedstefar's champion herd. Thank goodness nothing was mentioned about her.

Kirsten's cowardice and humiliation were not yet over. Shortly before her return trip to Copenhagen, the girl cousins biked down to one of the pastures. She could then say good bye to Musse, the mare. The girls went under the barbed wire, walked in, and called to Musse. The horse ambled over to the girls and eagerly nuzzled at their hands, searching for apple core, carrot, or a rye bread crust. Kirsten stroked the soft velvet of the horse's nose, and put her cheek along the muzzle, breathing in the smell of the horse—a smell she liked and wanted to remember.

Suddenly, she heard "Let's get out of here! Look at the herd of cows coming this way!" ....Too late, the cows were now between the girls and their exit. All, but Kirsten, made their way through them, under the wire and out to the road. She was once again frozen in fear of the cows. The other girls called and encouraged her. But, no matter what, she did not dare move. She stood, staring at more cows than she cared to be around. They stared back at her. Her cousins soon gave up and went for help. Once again, she was rescued by the hired hand when he entered the pasture and herded the cows out of the way, "I guess you will be happy to get back to Copenhagen," was his only comment.

*****

Kirsten never felt home sick and accepted she had to go back and join her family. She enjoyed the trip on the train while exchanging stories of summer events with all the other summer kids.

Upon her return home, it seemed to her she was a different person. *Maybe I feel all grown up now because I am ten years old.*

CHAPTER 20

She loved playing with Karl. He gave love and laughter back to her—chase and tickle, run and catch, hug and kiss, snuggle and cuddle—whenever Kirsten came home from school, he showed her how happy he was to see her. Kirsten babysat on the rare occasions both parents went out together. She felt important and loved the tranquility of her own little household. She often made French toast, without eggs—they were countable. She did not want to be found out. The gas stove didn't scare her. She knew how to strike a match, turn a button, and put the match to the burner. She did this at exactly the right time for it to light, without too big of a pop. She dipped the bread in milk then fried it in a little margarine. She flavored it with cinnamon and sugar. When she finished her special snack she made sure to clean up well. All Kirsten would do was admit to her mother she ate bread with a glass of milk. She thought it best not to mention she ate a bowl of sugar puff cereal or that she scooped spoonsful of syrup in her mouth.

*****

Ava and Erling entertained friends at the apartment early one evening before embarking on an evening booze cruise. They partook of liquid refreshments. Among these was a bottle of 'Prince of Denmark' wine. The name, the picture on the bottle, and the color of the liquid itself intrigued Kirsten. By the time the adults left, she knew no matter what, she was going to experience the taste of such a mystery.

Why did I pour it over the Ax-minster rug in the front room? Why didn't I carry it to the kitchen where I could easily wipe it up if I had to. The small spills of red wine dropped onto the cream colored background—not on one of the green leaves of the pattern.

Kirsten rubbed and rubbed—first with a dry rag and then with a wet one. Try as she might, the spot remained and it looked worse. The spot on the carpet was looking rather fuzzy after all the rubbing. Kirsten hated the taste. *If it was called 'Queen of Denmark' it wouldn't have been any better. Just like Eve, one bite of the forbidden apple, the same as one sip of the ruby red nectar and the day of reckoning was certain to come.* She was panic struck and started to grasp at ideas for an excuse.

Mum, Karl puked. No...won't work—puke is not red.

Mum, I was coloring my homework on the floor. My red crayon melted and went right through the paper, my hand was burning hot. No, it won't work, either.

After much agonizing, no matter which story she dreamed up, it would not matter why there was a stain on the carpet. The worst was it was there.

Kirsten decided to say she made a strawberry jam sandwich and how sorry she was for eating in the front room. After reaching this decision, she got on her hands and knees, and smelled the spot. Convinced her mother would smell the 'Prince of Denmark,' she went to the cupboard, got the strawberry jam and smeared it into the spot to make it authentic. Then she scrubbed with the wet dish rag. By now the stain looked much worse than the first go round.

She slept little that long night, waiting for them to come home from their dinner cruise between Denmark and Sweden.. *They will flip on the lights and see the spot right away.* She agonized . . .

*****

Home they came all right! They weren't seeing anything! A heated argument came with them!

"You danced and flirted like a two bit whore with any man who came along," Erling raged.

With sharp tongue Ava shouted, "Well I showed you? I am still able to attract other men besides you. All you do is sit there and get drunk. I want to have some fun, dance and feel desirable—if you would just get up and dance!"

"It was bad enough you danced with other passengers. But, I was so embarrassed when you grabbed the chef and dragged him out on the floor. Have you no shame?"

A volley of insults flew back and forth, sounds of pushing and shoving, slapping and weeping. Kirsten was not about to interfere. She lay rigid, squeezed Dolly Lise, and wept into her pillow. *Why was Mum talking about wanting other men?*

The next day, all day, was silent treatment day. The parents didn't even speak to the children. Kirsten felt sick with worry, anticipated more fighting, and the punishment yet to come for the carpet stain.

Days went by . . . Nothing was mentioned about the cursed spot. Ava cleaned it up somehow and only queried out loud as to what it could be, "Some people are so careless it's difficult to think adults slop like kids." Kirsten was much relieved to have gotten away scot free. She did not confess.

Kirsten always looked forward to the evenings when Gurli and Teddy came over. Gurli, the eldest daughter of Moster was happy and funny. She always fussed over the children, and brought a little treat for them each time. After little Karl was tucked in for the night, the adult foursome played cards and Kirsten was allowed to watch. They put money in the pot—the winner of the night got half, and the other half accumulated until the end of the winter season. At this time, the players enjoyed an evening out with the money from the pot.

The best part of the card playing nights was the deli made, open face sandwiches. Kirsten was allowed two of them when the adults took a break. Smorrebrod, the fancy open faced sandwiches, from a Deli, always tasted extra special. They looked like a real piece of art too, almost a shame to destroy by eating.

CHAPTER 21

Winter in Copenhagen is going to be boring again. No toboggan hill anywhere near— in Ribe, the banks of the moat, around the old castle grounds, provided the children there with hours of fun, sliding down and out onto the frozen water right out the back of their apartment.

So, it was with great pleasure that Kirsten went with Erling one Saturday to buy skates, and to go to the fancy skating rink. Her skates were shiny metal. They fit onto the bottom of her shoes. There was a special key used to tighten them on. Karin, Moster's youngest daughter took her a few times and Kirsten marveled at her fancy skates. The metal blade was attached to a white boot. Such a skate cost a lot of money. Karin only got them she said because her father felt guilty about being divorced from the family, and he lived with a pretty young thing.

*****

Erling found interesting items in the attic and the basement of the complex. He brought home an old black typewriter which he and Kirsten both started to toy around with. Another time he brought home a small wooden box. Inside were handles, attached by cords, and two wires and battery posts. The idea was to hang on to the handles while someone turned the dial and watched the meter to see how much current was going into the person hanging on. Kirsten never did know what good it did but it was rather fascinating. She and Erling took turns hanging on and getting buzzed.

They got their first telephone, black with gold trim. Once in a while they talked to Bedstemor and Bedstefar—never for long because it cost too much. Erling allowed Kirsten to phone one of her school chums just to see how it was done. In 1959, they got their first television. Kirsten looked forward to Saturdays when Robin Hood came on. The actors spoke English so she read the Danish subscript fast to follow along.

CHAPTER 22

Ava's moodiness and sharp tongue, and Erling's drinking and late nights caused tension in the household. Ava did not speak a lot, she wept often. Kirsten was hesitant to speak to her due to the sarcastic cold remarks that followed. As for speaking, to Erling—It didn't happen often. He was gone from home, on his bike, before Kirsten got up, and came home, most of the time, after she was in bed.

One evening, after her homework assignment was completed, Kirsten heard the door from the stairs close. She peeked into the front room to see who left. Erling was home so it was not him. It was her mother who vacated the apartment. "Where did Mum go?" Kirsten spoke softly.

The reply came just as soft and short, "She went out, window shopping."

Something was brewing in the air. Kirsten felt it for days. It all started when Erling came in the door, drunk and late, a couple of nights ago. As usual, Kirsten heard the pair fighting violently.

"I cook, I clean, and I mother. I am a damned slave around here—not enough money to go round, yet you go to the pub and blow cash which is needed here at home," Ava's voice higher and higher, faster and faster she yelled, "I made kale soup today, still in the pot on the cupboard. I am damn well on strike. It will sit there until it rots—no money, even for an ice block."

Rot, it did. The stench of rancid pork stock mixed with the strong odor of fermenting kale smothered the whole apartment, a few days later.

The kitchen sink was filled with dirty dishes and the counter littered with crumbs, milk spills, and dirty mildew reeking dish cloths, Kirsten decided she had been wrapped up in the nauseating smell long enough. *I must do something. I can't bear another day like this.* Kirsten's thoughts raced.

She knew what she must do and went into the filthy kitchen, and began the horrendous job of restoring cleanliness and tidiness. She emptied out the sink by stacking the dirty dishes on the cupboard, and then proceeded to dump the offensive brew into the sink. Gagging and choking, pausing once in a while, she turned away to gasp for cleaner air, and then faced the green slimy slurry again.

"What in the world is the noise all about? What are you doing out here? It's your bedtime," Erling chided.

"If Mum comes home to a clean kitchen, she will feel happy, everything will be all better." Kirsten didn't worry too much about saying this to Erling. He acknowledged most of her conversations with a grunt or a shrug. Sure enough, it worked as usual. He turned and went to his bed.

The sour soup was thick, difficult to run down the sink. Using a wooden spoon for stirring and running the tap all the while, the offensive concoction disappeared. The dishes were done, and put away. Kirsten, satisfied, went to bed, hopeful and exhausted. She did not hear or know what time her mother came home.

Next day, Kirsten waited for some sort of sign from her Mum, confirming happiness. When the sign didn't come, she got up enough nerve to broach the subject herself,

"Did you have a nice surprise last night, Mum?"

"If you mean about the kitchen—It's about time someone else cleaned things up around here besides me."

CHAPTER 23

When Kirsten brought home her report card, Ava checked to make sure her marks were high, and the teachers' comments favorable.

"This is exactly as it should be. You better make sure it stays this way or there will be hell to pay with me. I don't want a no-good stupid girl for a daughter."

Ava did not participate further in Kirsten's school activities or homework. Kirsten thought it nice of her classmates' Mums to take part, help out, and be in the audience for school concerts or plays. It didn't surprise Kirsten her mother was not interested. Anyway, Kirsten would have felt too nervous with her mother at school, and so she was allowed to blossom and grow under the encouragement and praise of her teachers.

One day Kirsten gave her Mum a note from Mrs. L'Orange and watched her face.

"What in the world does she have to come here for, sticking her nose into our business? What lies have you been telling at school?"Ava's eyes flashed with accusation.

"Mum, Mrs. L'Orange said to the class how much she would like to visit with all parents who could not get to school for parent teacher interview. I had to bring home the note. You are supposed to write down when she may come, and sign it. I have to give it to her tomorrow . . . I can't help it, I'm sorry."

The afternoon of the dreaded visit by Mrs. L'Orange, Kirsten was unable to concentrate at school. She did not eat lunch either. At recess, all she talked about to her friends was how worried she was, about the upcoming meeting.

What if Mum tells Mrs. L'Orange how bad I am and how often she has to get after me to make me be good. Kirsten worried what her teacher would think of her, after this visit.

Wrong, wrong—Oh happy day! Arriving home from school, Kirsten found her Mum looking pretty. The apartment was spick and span. A pound cake, fresh out of the oven, its smell wafting through the home, inviting and welcoming.

With her ear tight to the key hole, Kirsten strained to hear what the two women were saying as they visited over coffee and cake, in the front room.

"We are proud of Kirsten's marks. She is a good girl, a big help to me around the house with her younger brother. I am not aware of any problems at all where she is concerned."

Goody, goody, Mum is saying nice things. Everything is fine, nothing more to worry about. I am lucky.

Afterwards, Kirsten was allowed a piece of cake and a glass of milk even if it was just before supper. *Yes, Mum was nice today.* But, Kirsten pushed her luck a little too far when she asked about the possibility of a second serving of cake.

"You should not eat too much. It costs a lot of money to feed you. Do you want to get fat like the postman's daughter, Else?"

*****

One Sunday morning Kirsten asked her Mum, "May I please drink coffee?" "Whatever do you want coffee for? You don't drink coffee!"

"Well . . . I am going to start, and then I won't get fat," replied Kirsten, "instead of buying candy or bakery treats, I will buy little white tablets I saw in a magazine. If they are used in coffee it will help a person stay slim. I already bought some."

Kirsten was allowed a cup of coffee with her crusty bun breakfast. She thought her parents looked at each other in a strange way. *Are they making fun of me? They should be happy she was not going to get fat.* Kirsten did not enjoy the unfamiliar taste of coffee at all. Soon she forgot about her resolution.

CHAPTER 24

Christmas shopping in Sweden with Erling's cousin, Holger, turned out to be an embarrassing nightmare for Kirsten, not at all the happy adventure she imagined. There she was, accompanied by a police rookie, and bachelor. What a strange couple together on a shopping excursion, via the ferry, across to Sweden. It was not unusual for Danes to shop in Sweden. They got more for their money over there, in those days, something to do with the sales tax. Kirsten felt strange, alone with Holger.

She fantasized he was her big brother and how the other passengers would see them. Her dilemma began as soon as they set their feet on Swedish ground. If her mother was with her, she would long ago have expressed the need to visit a toilet, or her mother would have asked about such a possible necessity. To her, the topic of visiting a bathroom was one of those secrets—a topic almost as bad as 'The One Thing.' Kirsten believed she must hold it until she was back at home, in the apartment, in Copenhagen. To her dismay, she realized she could not hold it. She looked all around to see if she could spot a toilet. Danish and Swedish may be similar to some people but not to Kirsten. Panic overcame her shyness, when she felt the first damp warm trickle between her legs.

She pulled at Holger's sleeve and whispered, "Please . . . I need a bathroom?"
Nonchalant, Holger scouted around with his eyes, responded, and pointed, "There you go, right over there. I will wait right here." He gave her a little shove to get her going in the right direction. Away she hurried, thinking it wasn't too bad, asking him.

Kirsten entered the bathroom with almost dry underwear but horror of all horrors was about to be discovered. *I need money? No! No money!* Holger had her money. She heard only a foreign language spoken around her. *What am I to do?* A warm trickle again crept down her leg, soaking into her woolen leotards. She hurried, backtracking to Holger. Out of breath, she stammered, "I need money for the bathroom please!"

By the time she returned to the lady's bathroom all the cubicles were occupied. She stood in line suffering, and wet herself with no way of changing, or getting dry. Kirsten decided she could hide her embarrassment because she wore dark brown leotards and her skirt was over top. She hoped no one would smell the urine odor she smelled, and no one would know of the pee that had run into her shoes.

The shopping became a blur as anxious she was. She concentrated on getting to the ferry and getting home.

Holger said they would have supper on board. It meant she would have to sit on a leather seat, pressing her wet leotard into her dress, making a definite wet mark. The day got worse. The North Sea became its customary rough old self and Kirsten soon felt the first twinges of nausea right after telling herself not to get up. The food, in front of her, added to the surging nausea. She abandoned her wet spot on the leather. Without a word she dashed away from the table, reached the railing, just in time, to spew her vomit overboard.

Kirsten burst into tears the moment her mother opened the door, "How was the trip?"

Kirsten confided her disastrous ordeal to her mother, but came to regret it later. The story became the focal point of Ava's entertainment for quite a while. She thought nothing of sharing it with anyone.

*****

During the week before Christmas, Erling and Ava went out a few times and left Kirsten to mind Karl. Her curiosity got the better of her again. One evening, she got the step stool and set it up at her parent's tall wardrobe, with the intent of searching for presents. As she slid the top door open, it came off the slider. Gripped with panic, she discarded the thought of snooping and fought to return the panel to its tracks. Alas she could not manage it. She left it, looking as though it was in place.

She waited for the wrath to come but giggled with relief when one evening she heard, Erling, utter a curse, as the door panel clattered to the floor. He must have thought he caused the mishap, because he didn't mention it at all.

CHAPTER 25

Company came from America, actually from Canada which was in North America Kirsten learned. She was full of curiosity and excitement meeting Erling's two brothers, who were back in Denmark for a visit. They had been at her parents wedding but she did not remember them. She had seen pictures of them and pictures they sent home to their parents.

Fascinating pictures and slides of Indians, in full feather and leather dress— Cowboys swinging, digging in their spurs, atop bucking bulls and horses—Royal Canadian Mounted Police in splendid red uniforms— majestic mountain scenes with clear sparkling blue sometimes green water, and wildlife, moose, bear, deer, elk, and chipmunks.

They brought more pictures with them showing them standing beside their big fancy cars and in their nice modern apartment. Kirsten wasted no time in telling everyone she came in contact with that her two visiting uncles were rich indeed. On about the second day of the uncles' visit, Ava greeted Kirsten, after school, "How would you like to go to Canada?"

Kirsten was puzzled but excited, "It will be a great vacation! Wow, are we going to visit?"

"Who said anything about a vacation? We are moving there."

Kirsten's emotional peak of pleasure plummeted into a dark abyss, "No, no way, I'm not going! You can send me to live with Bedstemor and Bedstefar!" She fled to feed her fish, expecting Mum to chase after her and deliver a stinging slap.

Kirsten understood it was reckless talking back. She waited for her punishment but to her surprise, it never came. *How can they do this? Why must we move away? I will miss Bedstemor and Bedstefar. How will I ever find my real dad if I go far away?*

Later, at the evening meal, Kirsten heard more of the plans for the big move. The uncles painted a positive picture of life in Canada. Everyone owned a car and everyone could manage to buy their own home. Work was plentiful and easy to get. Life in Canada was easy going, not so much stress on formalities. The cost of living was a lot lower and it would be cheaper to buy everything in Canada—of course, cheaper than transporting belongings overseas.

Uncle John said, "Ava, you will soon be wearing a fur coat. All the women have one. They wear sneakers and fur coats at the same time and women wear slacks."

Kirsten listened with sadness. Not one person spoke to her. *How can they do this? Why must we move further away? How will I ever see all the special people in Ribe? What can I do about it?* She wept more tears, added more stains to Dolly Lise's aging cloth body.

Everything happened fast. Each day, after school, Kirsten saw signs confirming—the big move was inevitable. The furnishings started disappearing from the apartment. "Kirsten, see if you can sell your fish and the aquarium. You might as well help get some money together for this trip. If you can't sell it, you'll have to give it away. You can't take it with you. You know, don't you?" Ava was forever enforcing the fact of not taking anything.

Soon the family embarked on a trip to Jylland, the mainland, to say good bye to all the relatives—from the north to the south and in between. There were tears, and sadness, expressed by friends and family, never by the departing couple—they were happy and exuberant, eager to take their leave and set out for the new world.

Kirsten observed and kept silent. Karl was oblivious to the major change about to take place in their lives. He was too young to know and lapped up the loving attention of many well-wishing relatives. Four and a half years old, Karl was occupied talking about the airplane.

Soon, after arrival at the home of Erling's parents, Kirsten was presented with a farewell present meant to be of great help to her. The English-Danish dictionary was slim, red in color, and hard cover. She began to focus on her new possession. After all, it was going to Canada with her. *This English language is not going to be easy. Why don't letters sound out the same in English as they do in Danish? Why are there only twenty six letters in the English alphabet when the Danish one has twenty nine? How will I manage in school? Of course I should not fret because all the teachers in Denmark have learned some*

97

English. The teachers in Canada will surely speak some Danish. I will practice counting to ten, saying good day, farewell, please and thank you.

When Kirsten tried to learn the most important of all, she found 'tak for mad' meaning 'Thank you for food' was not even used. Instead the correct etiquette phrase to use after a meal was 'Please excuse me from the table.' She wondered if one was supposed to say it every time one sat at the table, even just when coloring? What about when one ate on a blanket at a picnic did one say, 'Please excuse me from the blanket?'

How final, the farewell was in Ribe and on the farm. When would Kirsten see her beloved relatives again? She thought maybe never again. To make matters worse, her mother informed her Dolly Lise would have to stay on the farm.

"The dirty doll is too big, takes up far too much room. Anyway you are getting too old to be clinging to a doll. At eleven years old, you should be ashamed, still cuddling a doll."

Bedstemor tried to help, "Little Kirsten, let's go find a safe, out of the way spot for Dolly Lise. When you come back, for a visit, you will find her there." Bedste guided her up the stairs by the tack room, they led into an attic storage space, "here we are and look. There is your little stuffed lamb."

Kirsten had forgotten about the lamb, now she recalled she had to leave it behind, when they moved to Copenhagen.

"Bedste, who, gave me the lamb?" Kirsten knew the lamb was somehow connected to her real dad from one of her eavesdropping sessions. She hoped Bedste would be open and honest with her.

"You know, I don't really remember. It must have been a good friend who wanted you to have something special."

Kirsten used to wrap her arms around the little lamb and gaze into the glass eyes. She would tap it on top of its head causing the lamb to nod up and down. Ava stated that the lamb was yellowed, dirty, and nothing but a moth attraction. It was not welcome in her household any longer. Kirsten knew it was useless to plead for any one of these precious friends. Her mother meant what she said. She was the boss.

Back in Copenhagen, all was in order for their departure. The last couple of nights they slept at Moster's apartment because their own was in turmoil. There was a lot of excitement in the air.

Kirsten and Karl got to go to a real movie theater. They saw a funny movie with a nutty actor, Jerry Lewis and a lot of rabbits. Kirsten told her brother they would have to learn to speak the same language because there wouldn't be any Danish text in Canada. The two of them practiced saying okay, no and yes.

Kirsten was given little tablets a few hours before going to the airport.

"We hope you won't be throwing up as usual," said her mother.

She hoped not either. Throwing up was not fun. She always felt so embarrassed, like on the ferry and the bus. The chastisement which always followed was not fun either. Kirsten had no idea of what it would be like in a plane. She wished they could travel to Canada by train. She never threw up on them.

The only bad thing that happened to her on a train happened the time she washed her hands after using the toilet and mesmerized stood helpless watching her silver ring—a birthday gift from Bedstemor and Bedstefar. It swirled around the sink, got sucked down the drain to land on the track below.

"You are a stupid girl," admonished her mother. Maybe some other little girl will find your ring and take better care of it than you did. It serves you right!"

*****

The time came. They stood posing for pictures at the airport. Her Mum's youngest sister was there with her fiancé. My poor sweet Auntie, Kirsten thought with compassion, for her weeping aunt who could not stop crying. Even her big sister's scolding did not stop her tears. Ava was annoyed with her sister and told her people were looking at her.

The family did not have a lot of luggage. They wore the clothes on their backs. Kirsten wore two sets—one on top of the other because there was no more room in their luggage which already contained one change each for when they reached their destination. There was a large wicker trunk with photos, the good china and Mum's best linen, as well as silverware. Kirsten carried a basket lined with material exactly as the dress one of her dolls wore. There were three dolls in the basket and these she was allowed to take. They were smaller than Dolly Lise, newer and cleaner and were not the kind for cuddling with. They were more like ornaments. She brought her favorite shooter marble and of course the little red, English-Danish dictionary, planning to study and learn more English.

*****

For Kirsten, the journey did not turn out well at all. A cut on her knee caused her pain and discomfort.

"Your own fault," said her mother, "Can you not sit like a lady instead of squirming and climbing around like a monkey in the jungle?"

Kirsten lapped up the stewardess' kindness. She watched intently as the stewardess administered first aid to her wound.

How pretty and well-dressed stewardesses are, maybe I will be one someday. I like their uniforms as much as the Salvation Army uniform.

Kirsten felt the disgusting symptoms, nausea and dizziness, creeping over her. Whenever this happened to her, she practiced the only defense she knew—*Sit still, with eyes fixed on a certain point, and concentrate. Don't talk to me. If they do, I have to answer and it just makes me want to puke even more.*

Ava, knowing the sign, observed, "Use the airsickness bag if you are going to vomit. It's right here, in the pocket of the seat, in front of you."

Sometime later, food trays were distributed among the passengers.

"If your tummy is feeling upset, eat a little soup it will make you feel much better," said the friendly stewardess. Kirsten moved her head, side to side, not speaking, so as not to feel sicker.

"Eat!" said her mother. Eat she did. Red soup, tomato soup, the first time she ate tomato soup. Soon she puked red soup with great force in no particular direction. As usual, the illness caused debilitating disorientation for the distraught girl. Puking in an organized respectful way was out of the question.

First, silence, disbelief, then grunts of disgust by the horrified onlookers. Surveying the scene, it was evident the main target hit by the liquid projectile, was Kirsten's own lacy pink doll basket—dolls included. Again the stewardess came to the rescue, smiling doing her best to help clean up the offensive mess.

A lot of hours passed before she was again encouraged to eat something. This time it was grapefruit sections, the first time she ever tasted the fruit. *Ech! It would be much better if it tasted like an orange.* It was bitter and the sugar on top didn't help. This time she managed to use the air sick, bag. *I will not make a good stewardess.*

Karl fussed. Erling and Ava were stressed and tired. To make matters worse, the captain's voice came over the speaker announcing the passengers should not worry. The flames shooting out from one of the propellers would soon be extinguished. Kirsten watched out the window, toward the wings and the propellers. She watched flames shooting out and then they disappeared. *Wow, I will really have stories to write about to everyone back home.*

After about twenty four hours, including stops in Greenland, London, and Toronto, to refuel, they reached their. Never in all her eleven years, had Kirsten ever felt so sleepy before. Karl was sleepy and whiny, too.

CHAPTER 26
CANADA 1960

It was a sunny bright day in Calgary. The travelers' biological clock, told them it was night time. Not having slept during the long travel hours made it even more difficult to stay awake.

Erling carried Karl, slung like a limp sack, over his shoulder, as they stepped off the plane, and onto the tarmac. Thank goodness, the stewardess held Kirsten's hand as they came down the steps because she felt she was about to tumble down.

She and Karl fell asleep on a bench, while their parents collected the luggage. After going through Canadian customs and immigration, they were greeted by one of Erling's brothers. Erling and the luggage rode with his brother. Ava and the children rode with the cabby. Lucky for Kirsten, Ava thought to bring an air sick bag, from the plane. This time, Kirsten managed to target exactly right into it—the back seat of cars always made her sick.

Kirsten wept when the first thing she was offered to eat on arrival was a half a grapefruit.

"I can't eat. I am too sick," she pleaded. It was impossible to keep the children up any longer. No matter it was breakfast time—Kirsten welcomed the single bed offered to her. She found blankets and sheets for covers confusing. She was used to duvets with covers like a giant pillow case—those, one did not tangle up in. She was used to a square pillow but snuggled with the oblong shaped one and immediately fell asleep.

She awoke in the dark room. *Where am I and why?* Soon, she realized, remembered the journey. All was quiet and dark in the house. No one stirred. Kirsten felt lonely, lost, and wide awake. She endured laying there for what seemed an eternity. *What will today bring me? How will I ever learn to speak English properly?* During the flight, she attempted some of the words she studied, in her little red book. The stewardesses did not understand one single word, when she tried asking how many hours were left until arrival.

*****

Aunt Elma and Uncle Ben were kind and hospitable. One day, soon after their arrival, Kirsten asked her mother if she thought she might be allowed to take a bath in the huge blue bathtub.

"Go ask Ben youself," her mother replied. Kirsten was nervous, shy. The tub beckoned to her. Finally she got up the nerve to approach Ben with her extravagant wish.

He chuckled with surprise and assured her she could take as many baths as she wished.

I feel like a movie star in this nice bubbly bath. We didn't have anything like this back home. She soaked until the water got cold.

Kirsten noticed many other differences between Denmark and Canada. She was awe struck by the newness of everything—New houses, new cars, new streets and side walk. Everything was bigger than back in Denmark. And, one could see a great distance in all directions.

Erling got a job right away as carpenter with a construction firm. The owners happened to be fellow Danish immigrants. Within a short time the family moved into a two bedroom apartment, in a building with five other suites. Her parents got the job as caretakers. Ava was happy.

"Dis vil be easy, not anyting like in Copenhagen."

It was decided Kirsten should not move with them, just yet, in order for her to learn how to speak English. Elma could not speak Danish. The two of them would have to get along the best they could. Kirsten would learn English out of necessity. She was introduced to young people in their neighborhood were Danish/English speaking. Elma allowed Kirsten the freedom to bake and clean house as she pleased. She enjoyed doing it for Elma who was late in her first pregnancy and was easy going, and praised her—even bought her a bathing suit as a reward. Kirsten was surprised and touched.

Kirsten had her first taste of watermelon, beef steaks as big as dinner plates and thick butter icing, on cakes. Her favorite new food was corn on the cob. *Just imagine, here in Canada they eat pig food, as it is known in Denmark.* Her least favorite new foods were instant potatoes, milk made from powder, and margarine, looking like lard—it was colored before using it. She really missed bread and buns as she knew, from back home. Bread in Canada was pure white fluff without varying texture, color and flavor.

The summer passed by quickly for Kirsten. It was time to move home to her own family and to begin school. She was a bit sorry to leave her new aunt, uncle, and new born, girl cousin. Besides getting along well with them, she became accustomed to the luxury of their new house and everything in it, including having her own room. The apartment was sparsely furnished. Family photos from Denmark decorated the walls in the living room. The only other piece of furniture, for a long time to come, was a wicker basket chair. For the kitchen, they got second hand, table and chairs. Most important—there was a refrigerator and made frozen Kool Aid pops. They were used to an ice box. Erling and Ava slept on a double mattress on the floor in their bedroom. The children however were not as lucky. For a few months, they slept between blankets on the hardwood floor and used cheap lumpy pillows. Both slept in the same room as they were used to but this was a nice big room with plenty of space for them. They soon established their own territories within it.

The family had the good china, silverware, and quality linen. Little by little the apartment filled. The children got beds, and Ava and Erling bought a second hand bedroom suite. Their spirits lifted with the arrival of each new item.

CHAPTER 27

They had arrived in Canada, June of 1960 and by September the same year it was time to go to school.

School was quite a struggle for both, Karl and Kirsten. After Karl ran away from school several times, it was decided to hold him back an additional year before starting the first grade. All the scolding and spanking did not make him mind. Karl did not falter. He even raced his mother, back to the apartment, after Ava took him to school twice in one day.

The teachers advised them the whole family must learn English, as soon as possible, and the best way would be to stop speaking Danish, no matter how difficult. Ava and Erling enrolled in a night course for immigrants and the family began the new language, as best they could. This turned out as sad advice—young Karl lost his first language. Ava and Erling developed a language all their own—a mixture of both languages with incorrect grammar, and patterns of speech which were not easily understood by either the relatives in Denmark or by Canadians. Erling soon dropped out of English class. Ava did give it her best but family and work made it difficult for her to go for long.

Part of Kirsten's duties in the evening was reading to Karl from primary readers, borrowed from the school library. As long as there were pictures to look at Karl did not mind. As she read the story of the Three Little Pigs, Erling, with great disapproval, put down the newspaper and gave a demand as to what she was reading. The word pig was like the Danish word pik, used when talking crudely about a penis. Both Erling and Kirsten blushed, getting through the explanation—it was not to talk about.

Erling learned most of his English on the job some of which was not suitable for family conversation. One Sunday afternoon there were visitors and the adults were deep in conversation. Erling tried out an exclamation. Edith, a guest, asked if he knew the meaning of what he just said as she whispered the question to him.

"No oh . . . I guess I don't know," Erling turned quite red. Next day at school Kirsten found out what F-U-C-K meant when she asked a friend.

"Oh, here they have one word for 'the one thing.'" Kirsten never did learn just one word for it in Danish.

She giggled a little to herself, every morning, when in the classroom the students said the Lord's Prayer—lort in Danish sounded much the same but meant S-H-I-T.

A lot of immigrant children were set back one grade at school, when first they arrived in Canada. Kirsten was already much older than her peers, in her grade, therefore she continued with grade five as she would have done in Denmark. There, children must reach the age of seven, before starting school. In Canada some children started at age five. The whole school year was full of hurdles. Kirsten's first report card was all D's and C's. In those days, H for honors was tops, followed by A's, then

B's and so on with all the plusses and minuses in between. At first, the best she could do was simply sit and listen to lectures she did not understand, and copy notes, from the black board, which didn't mean much to her either.

Her teacher insisted her name was pronounced 'Kursten' now because she lived in Canada, and not 'Kiersten'. Her classmates nicknamed her 'Curse.'

When she changed schools going into Junior High she changed her name again. "Please call me Chris," she asked of everyone including her family.

Years later, whenever a legal document was drawn up she used her real name. She regretted giving up the sound of it. In time, she changed the spelling of Chris to Kris—at least it was the correct initial.

Kirsten hoped for acceptance by the girls at recess. She used to stand against the wall of the school, watching them skip. She was a good skipper and wanted to be invited to join in. One girl approached her after being prompted by the teacher on supervision. She tried hard to chant along with the rhymes the girls sang to skip by. She thought she mastered them in her head just fine, when she stood observing. It was a great let down for her at the next recess when she was told, "Sorry, but you speak and sing funny. You make us lose our step. We don't want you," they giggled as they walked away.

Kirsten was on the verge of tears but fought to keep them unnoticed. She shrugged her shoulders, and gave the girls a 'couldn't care' less, smile, then turned on her heel and sauntered off. She read and studied during recesses after that and determined to speak fluent English without a trace of her Danish accent. She was accustomed to trying hard to please others for recognition, and her perseverance paid off. By grade six, Kirsten got H and A's at report time. Accepted and sought after, by her peers, she was no longer, the new "DP." English was as easy for her as her discarded mother tongue.

If ever there was a time Kirsten would remember her mother as happy and content—not too angry or verbally abusive—this was the time.

The family kept getting ahead. It was not long before they got their first car, a black Chevrolet. They went on picnics in the summer and trips to explore the magnificent beautiful mountains. Kirsten liked eating French fries for the first time, and drinking milk shakes so thick the straw stood in the middle. They especially savored deep-fried chicken from 'Chicken on The Way.' It seemed they enjoyed a rich luxurious life in the new world. They loved winter adventures too, like the trip to Chestermere Lake with the toboggan behind the car. To think, ice in Canada froze hard enough and thick enough to withstand a car being driven on it. Yes . . . there were some good times . . .

CHAPTER 28

To belong—Kirsten's first and foremost challenge. She wanted to establish roots, find someone, something to fit in with. At Knob Hill Elementary school, she became friends with a Jewish girl, Esther. They were both school safety patrols. Each Saturday morning, they attended 'Safety Round Up' at the Palace Theatre, in downtown Calgary. Esther was talented at singing. She was soon on stage, performing, before the movie they were treated to. She always wanted Kirsten to sing with her. Either Esther needed company, to feel confident, or she was just being kind to Kirsten with no voice ability at all.

"So what if you don't sound right when you sing alone? You sound fine when you sing with someone," Esther said.

Soon they were on the Ed Hunter Children's Show, singing. Ester belted out the words, Kirsten sang along in a subdued voice.

Her parents must have felt proud, because they took a picture of the television screen and sent a picture to Bedstemor.

Esther came to spend Christmas Eve with them. Her family celebrated Hanukkah in strict Jewish tradition. Canada is country with a lot of different types of people celebrating events differently. In Denmark, all families celebrate the same—on Christmas Eve—the food and of course gift opening.

Kirsten was thrilled to open exactly what she wished for—a chenille bedspread with flowers, for the bed she now slept in, a fuzzy mat to put on the floor beside her bed, and a lamp to hang on the wall above her bed. Now she could read at night.

The girls were good buddies, and started sleep overs at each other's home, until an upsetting occurrence happened—something not to talk about. Kirsten made excuses not to go to Esther's house anymore, and never told Esther the reason why, or anyone else. She was too ashamed to tell, and worried she was to blame. *It's best to forget about it and Esther.*

Kirsten did not utter one single word that miserable day. Esther was taking a bath and Kirsten was engrossed in a comic as she lay on Esther's bed. She looked up and saw her friend's father with a smile on his face and a finger to his lips which made her feel puzzled. He sat himself on the bed beside her and whispered, "I am happy you are my daughter's good friend. You are a sweet little girl," he said as he placed his whole hand on Kirsten's newly budding, developing breasts and squeezed and caressed them. She felt stunned, sick inside and frightened. He continued with, "I like it when you come to my house. I will always be nice to you. Would you like to sit in my lap? We will hug each other."

Kirsten never got out an answer. Lucky for her, Esther yelled from the bathroom,

"I will be out in a minute, and then you can take your turn."

She stayed her last night in Esther's house. But, she could not explain to Esther, nor, could she go home and explain. She survived the night by not being alone anywhere where he might come touching her again.

She thought of her Mum being right—men only wanting one thing. She dared not confide in her Mum.

CHAPTER 29

The subject of boys was saved for discussion with girlfriends or for her own private thoughts. One of her girlfriends shared her stories about her parent's obviously happy fun sex life. Kirsten was surprised to hear about how these people giggled and exulted through it—the one thing. To please her parents, Kirsten behaved as though she thought boys to be second class citizens and was not the least bit interested in them.

When she was invited to a birthday party she didn't mention to her parents it was a boy/girl event. They played spin the bottle and post office—silly kissing games which caused Kirsten guilt feelings. She didn't like kissing all the boys. She went along because the other girls didn't seem to mind.

One of the boys asked her to a Saturday afternoon movie and her heart kind of skipped a beat. They were to go on a double date. She didn't tell her parents. Instead she asked them if she and a girlfriend could go to a movie.

"You may go but you have to take Karl."

The other kids didn't mind her little brother coming along. They all met at the theatre and Kirsten made it look like a coincidence to have run into them.

Age twelve and on her first real date, with a boy named Richard, sitting on one side of her, and her brother Karl, age seven, sat on her other side.

During the movie, Richard put his arm on the back of her chair. He let his arm slide, his fingers rested on her shoulder.

Later back home in the apartment, Karl blurted out,

"Guess what everybody—There was a boy sitting next to Kirsten at the movie today. I think he liked her, na, na, na, na."

Kirsten was gripped in fear. *What was to come next?* She shot her little brother a threatening glance. She warned him if he told, he would never again come with her.

"Ha! Mum and Dad will make you take me anyway," taunted the smug boy.

Lucky for her, her parents did not get the real picture of Karl's teasing. They must have thought it was just any boy, unknown to their daughter. Kirsten hoped boys didn't want 'the one thing.' Maybe it was only grown up men who did, she wondered. Kirsten was starting to believe this to be true. It was not just Esther's father who behaved that way toward her.

While still living in the apartment, one of her parents' single friends, stayed over, on the living room couch after drinking with Ava and Erling. On one such occasion, he entered the children's' bedroom and woke Kirsten, shaking her shoulder.

"Please find me a blanket to cover with. I'm freezing."

"Sure Okay, there is a blanket in the closet, right there beside the couch, you can get it," Kirsten was happy to solve his discomfort. She really liked him. She thought he looked like a movie star and he always teased her with compliments which flattered her.

He mumbled how he could not see in the dark and then, "Please come help me, I'm cold," there was a strong odor of liquor on his breath.

Oh, he is drunk I guess I better help. Kirsten wearing baby doll pajamas felt a little shy but knew he probably was drunk and he would not notice. Out of bed, into the front room she went, picked out the blanket and turned around to see him already lying down.

"Please cover me up," he begged.

Obliging, she spread the blanket out over him. He grabbed her hand,

"Lay here with me until I warm up? You are cute, come on, little one."

Kirsten froze for just a moment, then adrenalin kicked in as she heard the warning words, silent, inside her head, *men only want one thing, stay away from them.* She snatched her hand away from his,

"NO, she said, No!" and rushed to her room, hoping he would stay away. Nothing was ever mentioned by the young man or herself

.

*****

Kirsten's puppy love for Richard caused her to behave like a fool. She stood in a dreamlike state at the bus stop, then using her house key, she set to work and KT+RB was carved there on a post along with other's initials for the whole world to see. If she realized the anxiety she just caused herself, she would not have acted on such an impulse.

Whenever, she went to the bus stop with her mother, afterwards, she was gripped with fear. *Will Mum notice what I have done?* Kirsten stood in front of the post, talked a mile a minute, and pointed out how nice the flower bed over there, or how ugly a house color was. *When Mum takes the bus without me, then what?* She rehearsed a lie in her head many times just in case it was needed—*Oh, it makes me mad. Kids have teased me about and it's not even me! There is a girl named Karen Thompson, (she did not exist) she lives over in the next block. Those initials are hers and I don't even know the boy.* The lie was never needed.

CHAPTER 30

Sharon, another new friend, whose mother liked 'the one thing' or at least Sharon thought she did, talked to Kirsten about YWCA camp at Sylvan Lake. Kirsten hoped to have such an experience. Thinking negative thoughts about how remote her chance for permission—too expensive, and how she was needed at home—she bravely broached the subject anyway.

How wonderful! What luck! Oh happy day! I'm off to camp. She did not get into the same cabin as Sharon but, soon eight girls, unknown to each other before, were chatting together, while they settled in.

Prestige among the girls ranked highest for those who already had the monthly curse as the girls called menstruation. Now, Kirsten hoped she would never be called 'Curse' again, and she didn't mention how it was once her nickname. There were only two girls who had not yet bloomed into womanhood.

One of the girls in Kirsten's cabin, who had not yet menstruated, felt the need to lie about her maturity in a most peculiar fashion. A sanitary pad was left exposed, unfolded, and smeared in red. This greeted all the girls' eyes as they filed into their cabin. It was revealed later—it was ketchup.

Why was the girl in a hurry in promoting such an unhappy event? Kirsten felt sorry for the girl. It had only happened twice to her and she was not impressed by the inconvenience of it all. She had discovered it in the bathroom and had yelled to her mother,

"It's here! The bloody thing is here! What do I do now?" Ava came offering a rag.

"I can't be using this. I want Kotex. My friends use Kotex."

"Rags have been good enough for me all dese years," Ava started, but for some reason or other she took pity on the now crying girl and said no more. The next day she offered a sanitary belt and Kotex pads.

"You know, Kirsten, you may not swim or take a bath during your period. Get used to sponge bathing like we did in Denmark."

CHAPTER 31

After she graduated from Knob Hill Elementary School to King Edward Junior High School, boys could not be ignored. Chris, using her new name, was by now thirteen but looked a lot older. She did not hang out with her much younger class mates nor did she enjoy the classroom sock hops with them either. Most of the boys reached only to her shoulders. Their noses lined up perfectly with her developed bust line.

She struck up friendship with a fifteen-year old girl, Hilda. They met walking to and from school. She let herself be led by Hilda who was adept at fixing hair dos and applying make-up. Chris never gave her parents the opportunity to get to know Hilda who was quite boy crazy.

She told her parents she was attending s sports tournament at school on Friday night and there was a sock hop afterwards, chaperoned by teachers and would they please say yes to her sleeping over at Hilda's. She didn't ask Hilda to a sleep over at her house—she didn't have her own room.

There were no sports tournament and no sock hop. There was a teen dance, at the South West Calgary Community Hall with a real live dance band. With Hilda's touch, Chris looked much older with teased high hair, darker foundation to resemble a tan and pale pink lipstick. Hilda introduced her around a bit at first but she was a wall flower, at the sidelines, sitting on a chair, looking on. Hilda was popular. She jived and waltzed with several different boys. Hilda won dance contests and spot prizes. In between, she disappeared into the dark end of the hall where couples sat and necked. Each time Hilda went to the bathroom she came looking for Chris.

"Did anybody ask you to dance yet? Are you having fun? Don't be shy! Don't you know how to dance?"

Hilda wasted no time in giving her jiving lessons. She caught on fast—thanks to dance class in Ribe—she had a good sense of rhythm.

At the next teen dance, Hilda introduced her to a guy, clumsy and bookish looking. He asked her to dance with him after Hilda told him he should.

When the band took a break, he held her hand and led her to the back of the hall where he tried to kiss her. Chris was repulsed, made excuses, and left him standing there.

Meeting Hilda in the bathroom, she blurted out, "I think the guy is a creep! I don't want to spend any more time with him! He tried to stick his tongue in my mouth when he kissed me! It was awful!"

Hilda just laughed, "Have you not heard of French Kissing? Everybody does it. You will learn to like it. Don't worry."

"Not I! I will not be going to the back of the hall again, with any boy, no matter whom."

After the dance, Hilda gave more lessons—this time about kissing.

"Apply lipstick, kiss the mirror, and see how perfect a puckered rosebud, slightly parted, you can kiss."

It was fun, but Chris did not intend to practice it on a real live boy. Hilda had a lot of magazines: True Story, True Confession and others. Gone were the days of comics. Hilda encouraged her to read all these romance stories, "These will teach you a lot. They will help to get you in the mood for necking."

Chris developed a crush on a different boy each week or two—Boris, Don, Malcolm, and not to forget, Doug, a guitar player in one of the bands. During one of their breaks, records played, and he asked Chris to dance. She was relieved when he didn't try taking her to the back of the hall to neck. At the end of the evening he asked her to go steady. She was flattered and said yes.

Doug lived at the other end of Calgary. They would not see each other until two weeks later, back at the same hall. She was proud to have a ring on a chain, around her neck, to show off, and she impressed Hilda. Two weeks later, Chris gave Doug his ring back. She told him her parents did not allow her to go steady. Hurting Doug's feelings was not what she wanted nor did she want the relationship to get to the necking stage.

She handled relationships with other boys much the same way. She enjoyed cuddling on the dance floor. She liked getting them hooked but backed out while everything was still safe.

Hilda warned her she was going to be known as a tease, "don't you know boys suffer with pain when a girl teases?"

Chris didn't fall for such an explanation—didn't understand what it meant—She didn't care if they were in pain. She was afraid to experience petting. To go any further than kissing was against her values. She was fearful of her mother's wrath, if her mother found out all she was doing. It was bad enough for her if her mother found out about the lies, and the makeup. Hilda's influence and encouragement about boys would bring on the worst of punishment, from her parents. Chris thought it was her good fortune her parents did not take much of an interest in her. She found it easy to mislead them.

She became friends with two other girls, through Hilda. Donna and Ina were somewhere in between Hilda and Chris, in age. These four girls wanted to be accepted by the group of kids living in the Mount Royal district. The girls from Mount Royal were quite snobby and stayed in their own clique. They did not make friendly overtures to the four girls, who came from the neighborhood on the other side of the school. The boys however were not discriminating. Thanks to them, the four girls got invited to parties, in the big rich homes.

Donna lived with her parents in a small apartment. They both worked and Donna, an only child, spent a lot of hours alone. Ina lived with her divorced mother. Her brother lived with their father, and Ina also spent a lot of time alone. With Hilda as their leader, the four girls formed a little clique, all their own. They devised a way to have their freedom on spring week ends. Since none of the parents knew each other—nor even lived near each other––it was no problem for the girls to pull the wool over their parents' eyes. They were at a sleep over, at one or the other's home, as far as their parents' knew. It was uncanny how they never got caught in this deception. The girls roamed the streets, through the night, hanging around in parks or crashing boys' back yard tenting parties.

They hung out at a friend's house whose parents were away for the week end. The kids would get their kicks from phone pranks and 'Knock a Door Ginger.'

A close scare came after crashing a camp out at Steve's house. The girls made a mad dash when a parent turned the outside lights on and asked what was going on. This pumped the girls' adrenalin and set their legs into action. Through the hedge they shot, like wild cats on the run. They reached the school yard, where they intended to hang out when they noticed a police cruiser driving along slow.

"Too late, here they come," said Hilda, "now act normal and don't be nervous."

"What are you girls doing out at this time of night?" asked the officer from his rolled down window.

"We just finished babysitting. We are on our way home."

"Would you like a ride then?"

"No thanks, sir. We are almost home," Hilda the spokesperson was convincing.

The girls carried on to an early morning coffee shop. They enjoyed their favorite food—French fries with gravy and banana cream pie.

With the end of grade seven it was time for Chris to accept another change.

CHAPTER 32

Many called her by the name of Christine. *If only the teachers and the kids at school would have been kind enough to learn to pronounce my name the way it is in Danish. If only, the nickname 'Curse' hadn't become my tag.*

But, now they won't call me DP—no accent. I speak English just as well as the rest of them and I'm in the top of my class with my marks. If only I was not much older than the rest of my class mates. I will still be explaining how in my old country one had to be seven to start. I will not have them thinking I failed two grades— worse than if it were known she was an immigrant. All this went through her mind before going to her new school.

The family moved into a brand new house in a new district.

Ava and Erling made a lot of new friends, through clubs, formed by immigrant Danes, and enjoyed the circle of parties that were held. Some of these immigrants were like new relatives to the family.

Whisky had become the drink of choice—even Ava who had not drank often—now enjoyed Rye and 7UP. On New Year's Eve Chris happened to see her mother passed out on the bathroom floor after Erling brought her and Karl home from a friend's house where she babysat lots of children. She felt scared for her mother's well-being but the intoxicated Erling, more talkative than normal, assured her Mum had too much of a good time. There was no fight. All remained quiet.

Chris went to bed troubled for a different reason—an obscene phone call came to the place where she spent the evening baby-sitting. She never wanted to sit there again. She wondered how to prevent it because she was much too ashamed to bring it out in the open. It was not to talk about.

*****

Ava became pregnant, an accident, but miscarried. Chris heard about this while eavesdropping. Ava was pregnant again.

A sister, Wendy, was born. She was a real beauty, adored by her siblings. Chris was put in charge of caring for the newborn. Mum returned to work for the night shift at the nursing home because the family needed the money.

The infant cried a lot. Ava complained about her crying and didn't seem to be able to soothe the little one. Chris knew how much Mum hated anyone crying. The more one was told to quit bawling, the more one needed to cry. The agony of swallowing the lump or hiding tears was an ordeal for Chris, herself. It was even more dreadful for her, when one of the younger children were bullied, by the parents, to stop crying. She wanted to protect them, guard them from evil anger and longed to put her arms around them, cuddle them, and wipe their tears. This was not allowed either. But, sometimes, on the sly, she managed to comfort them.

One day, Karl came in crying. A bully, outside, hit him. Erling gave Karl a lesson.

"Hit back! Give him a good one—Hard! He'll learn to respect you and learn to leave you alone! Be a man, not a sissy! No crying! Only girls cry, boys don't."

In the evenings, Erling gave Karl instructions and made him practice how to make a proper fist then battled with the impressionable Karl.

Chris, on occasion, helped Karl out. She didn't like to fight or be mean to anyone, but she became enraged, to see Karl hurt.

Soon, Karl was fighting all the time, with his playmates. Their parents came to complain to Ava about her son and his mean streak. This was hard on Karl, the poor little tyke—first in trouble for not fighting back, and now, he was in trouble for fighting.

*****

On nights when baby Wendy cried a lot and Ava happened to be home, she verbalized her displeasure loud and clear, making it difficult for others to sleep. Chris often woke and felt fearful Ava would do the baby harm— Ava and Erling both had short tempers. On a particular bad night—Wendy was only three months old—Chris witnessed her mother shaking the baby hard and yelling at her. Later in the early morning, Wendy still crying, Kirsten heard her mother yell,

"I can't take dis anymore!"
Erling jumped out of bed and then Kirsten heard Erling spank the little one and yell,

"Stop it! Will you stop it? Stop it!"

Poor little Wendy cried, held her breath—continued to cry.

Chris held her breath, afraid to do anything. She cried and vowed hatred for her parents. From then on she tried to get to Wendy first, whenever she woke in the night.

Once, when she slept through the crying, Erling appeared at her bedroom door and in stern voice, chastised,

"Get up. You are a lazy girl! Your Modder is tired from vorking, needs her sleep. You take care of Wendy." He went off to work.

Chris' care giving duties increased after they moved into the new house. Through the summer, she babysat her siblings while her parents worked. She did not have any free time but it didn't matter because she had not made many new friends, except one girl next door. This girl was older and would not be going to the same grade or school as Chris. The two girls baked together a few times.

While strolling on the side walk with Wendy in the pram, a neighbor approached her and asked if she did any babysitting for other families.

"Well, a little, but not much right now because I am too busy at home."

"I have watched you with your own little baby and thought you would be a good sitter for my kids."

"This is my sister, not my baby!" Chris felt weird about the implication.

"Oh excuse me! How old are you? You look old enough to have one of your own."

"I am fourteen," replied Chris. "And, excuse me, I better get home now."

CHAPTER 33

At age fourteen, boys and girls in Denmark were usually confirmed in the Lutheran church. There, it was a special event for the young person. It ranked right up there next to a wedding. Christenings were important. At times such as these, relatives and close friends came together in great numbers, dressed in their finest, bringing gifts, and singing songs about the honored one. The host family put lots of time and expense into planning and preparation. The food was always scrumptious, presented in a formal way, and served on the best of china and linen.

Before a confirmation took place the conformant must attend religious lessons for a specified amount of time. Ava informed Chris she and Wendy would be done the same day—there was a visiting pastor from Denmark on vacation in Canada.

"You are lucky dat dey vil make an exception to deir rule. You vil attend a few short hours of instruction and den get confirmed," Ava said.

Chris' understanding of the whole process was confirmation was a ritual—a tradition, declaring her an adult. Christening babies insured they would go to heaven instead of hell—it was not good to wait long before christening a baby—in case it died early and the poor thing went to hell. A good thing little Kaj was Christened thought Chris. She was happy to think of him as a cute little angel playing his harp. Chris thought often about him, as she lay in bed, thinking 'if only' thoughts.

Ava and Chris went shopping for Chris' confirmation dress. Most were too expensive, some were inappropriate for such an occasion. One was just right— pure white, two layers in the skirt and the top one was lace—scratchy lace. Bell sleeves gathered with a bow just above the elbows. Chris thought the dress was as beautiful as any bridal gown and in anticipation of wearing the dress she looked forward to the confirmation. She recalled the dress worn at Ava and Erling's wedding and thought there was a similarity. One big difference though, she was a child then. Now she felt she was an adult.

The ceremony of confirmation and christening went rather fast. All filed outside Sharon Lutheran Church for picture poses. There was a reporter from the Calgary/Danish newspaper. Chris held baby Wendy in most of the poses. Wendy wore the special family heirloom gown, hand stitched by great-grandmother Kirsten Marie for the first born child of Bedstemor Emma. Ava as first born took great pride in informing all of this great significance. The gown was sent over from Denmark and it would be returned for future off spring of the family tree over there. Back at the house, everyone gathered around to watch Chris open her presents. When she opened her gift from all the relatives in Denmark her tears nearly spilled over. She fought for control knowing her mother would be embarrassed and angry if she cried in front of all these people. The gift was a Royal Copenhagen porcelain vase. Chris stroked the smooth cool vase and held it to her cheek and wondered whose loving hands last touched it before it was sent. She visualized it was Bedstemor. Chris looked down at her wrist—at the watch her Oldemor willed to her, for her confirmation gift. Ava gave it to her a year earlier because she thought she may as well, not knowing if she would be confirmed at all since they did not attend church. Chris was proud of the watch with the mother of pearl face and it gave her a feeling of having been important to someone. Often she looked at the picture of Oldemor holding her up in her arms. Chris put it into her picture album. Her only memory of the old lady was the kale soup she served. It was made with oats. Little Kis did not like it one bit.

A fancy table with all the traditional foods for Smorrebrod—the delicious open-faced sandwiches—was decked out. Chris enjoyed the early part of the meal until most of the adults got drunk and then the party seemed to be for them. She withdrew to her room and let her mind go into 'if only' thoughts'. She fantasized about how her confirmation in Denmark would have been with all her relatives attending, including her real father—recently found—a fantasy for sure.

CHAPTER 34

Nervousness in the highest degree consumed Chris as she started out for David Thompson Jr. High School. She

NOT TO TALK ABOUT—UNTIL NOW

hoped the yellow flowered, print dress, with the flared skirt was right for her first day at her new school.

Chris was pleased with her new wardrobe. She had grown and developed quickly and none of her old clothes fit. Her mum's friend, Gudrun, a seamstress, agreed to make her new outfits. She was talented at dress making. Everything felt and looked wonderful on Chris. Besides the yellow dress there were two others. One was a red dress, slim cut with a short jacket. The other was a black, slim fitting, belted dress with a cowl collar. Chris herself purchased a green pleated skirt and print blouse with her babysitting money and Mum got Gudrun to sew a grey narrow skirt for them both. Chris bought a grey sweater and a neck scarf to go with the skirt. Ava was pleased with Chris' appearance. She even seemed proud whenever she made Chris model in front of Ava's other friends and lapped up the compliments about how her daughter certainly got her looks and figure from her.

Confident in her appearance but still butterflies multiplied and danced out of control. At change of class room time Chris found a watch on the desk she was to occupy. She went to the front and brought it to the teacher's attention. He asked her to take it from room to room and find its rightful owner. Chris did not feel enthusiastic about doing it. *Why, Oh why did this happen to me. I won't be blending into the crowd this way!* She did not wanted to offend the teacher by saying no. She felt on display, especially when she entered 8b. A boy in the back row raised his arms, whistled at her and shouted, "mine, it's mine." It was not his but he drew attention to himself.

Chris felt flattered and excited by his attention, which surprised her. There was something a bit familiar about him and she realized she had seen him a few times before.

Can't be him . . . the same boy I saw at SW Calgary dances, the one who often danced with Hilda? ...He could not be here! Hilda talked about him. He was much older and in high school...Must be a younger brother, maybe? Chris saw this same person she was quite sure, walking down a sidewalk, as she went by in the car with Erling one day in the summer. Her heart jumped a little as she admired him through the window. She pushed the thought away as she headed back to her class, 8a.

*****

Chris became acquainted with her fellow students, and no question of acceptance at all this time. It was a fairly new school surrounded by new communities so most students were new to each other and all wanted to bond together. Chris walked to and from school with girls in her own neighborhood and became close with Diane. The two girls began a friendship that would blossom into a lifelong relationship.

After commencement of the school year, Chris was invited to attend a coed party at Heather's house. She was surprised that her parents' allowed her to go. They even hired a baby sitter to make it possible. They were going out too. Ava said, "Vel dis one time we vil do dis. You can have a chance to make friends but from now on vee are making rules that you must obey," Ava proceeded with the details, "you may go out with friends, one Friday or

Saturday night each second veek end. You have to be home by eleven o'clock and you don't go out until Vendy is bathed and ready for bed. Make sure de dishes are done too before you go."

Chris felt excited and happy to escape, full of anticipation for the party. She arrived before anyone else. Heather suggested that they take a walk to the corner to see if anyone was around to invite over to her house. She wasn't sure who would show up later.

A black Volkswagen pulled up to the curb, with a couple of guys in it. Heather knew them and she leaned in the passenger window and chatted. Chris hung shyly back, feeling apprehensive with what seemed a pickup situation. *Oh my God... It's him!* Chris startled inside.

"Come on, Chris. Let's hurry back to my place. These guys are goanna pick up a few more friends and then come over," Heather tugged at Chris' arm and away they went.

"I think I know one of those guys, the passenger. I think I saw him at SW Calgary community hall, dancing with my friend."

"His name is Eddy, he's okay. His friend is John. At least we'll have someone to dance with. Come on help me pick out records before they get here."

Later in the evening Eddy asked, "Want to dance?"

"Sure," Chris accepted and joined him for a slow dance.

"Hey, are you the girl with the watch the other day at school?"

"Ya, and aren't you the guy from the back row lying about owning the watch?" Chris teased.

"Uh huh, I just wanted to get your attention because I never saw you before. You must be new around here," Eddy explained.

"Do you tell fibs a lot to get attention, like at South West Calgary Community Hall dances?"

Eddy stopped leading the dance and they stood still, "what do you mean?"

"I have a friend by name of Hilda, you know her I think? Well you might not have seen me before but I have seen you at a teen dance in my old neighborhood." Chris followed Eddy to a seat on the chesterfield.

"Oh, gees, I'm caught good aren't I? The truth is I flunked grade one and grade 3. School just isn't my thing. I look forward to getting out and take a trade. I don't like sitting in a classroom with kids younger but smarter than me."

"I don't much like being older in class either. I come from Denmark and there you have to be seven before attending school. My birthday is in May and by September I was well on my way to eight. It was okay there because that's how it was but here some of my class mates were still five when they started."

"I thought you looked older than most in our grade. Come on let's dance," he reached for her hand and they jived quite well together. They danced together the rest of the short evening and Chris got a ride home in the Volkswagen. Eddy kissed her while they sat in the back seat. Chris was overwhelmed and surprised by how she felt. She floated into the house. Never before in her life, had she felt anything this intense. She cuddled her pillow and drifted asleep.

CHAPTER 35

Elections were held for the student council. Chris was amazed when she was nominated to run for office of social convener. Flattered and determined to do her best she got into making placards and campaigning. Rallies and public speaking, including debates, took place in the school auditorium. Eddy won as president, his brother, Ric, vice president, and Chris, for the position as social convener. The other positions such as secretary and treasurer were filled by students competent at those tasks. Chris looked forward to meetings of the council and working with Eddy but fate interfered.

Chris dipped her hair into the purple water, in the bathroom basin, planning for a hint of platinum in her blonde locks, when her Mother yelled out, "Dere is somebody at de door for you." Chris grabbed for a towel and wrapped her hair out of sight. Her heart almost leaped outside herself when she caught sight of Eddy in the doorway. She felt happy about the fact he came to see her but she seized with frenzy at imagination of what wrath would descend upon her because he came. Of course, Ava did invite him in. Chris greeted him in an unusual manner and recognized his bewilderment at not being invited in. She dared not.

"May I have your address and phone number?" Eddy asked. "I am going away to school and will be living in Debolt, up north, at my aunt's, by Grande Prairie," He informed.

"Why? How come? What about council and all?"

"Oh, everyone thinks it's best," Eddy tried to brush away the subject when Ava yelled out in her rudest voice.

"Shut de door dere's a bad draft you better get in now!" Chris rushed to give Eddy her address and phone number and said how sad she was that he was leaving and shut the door in his face.

"Who was dat boy? You make sure dat you don't make a habit of having him or any odder boy hanging around here!" Ava reprimanded.

"Oh he's just someone from school—you know— from our student council, he's moving away and gave me instructions about a council project."

"Good, as long as he is moving away. Good riddance!"

*****

Shit! What a disaster! Chris saw her hair a deep purple, when she took off the towel. The platinum rinse was meant to be on the hair for a couple of minutes. *How long was it on?* She shampooed several times without noticeable change. She was depressed about Eddy and her hair too. She went to bed feeling pure misery.

In the morning Ava laughed when she saw her daughter's hair.

"I can't go to school like this! I can't!" Chris lamented.

"Vel, see what you can do about it. Stay home dis morning, you go dis afternoon."

"Chris tried dish soap, laundry soap, and hand soap. Her hair did not lose the lilac color but no choice, off to school she went. Her home room teacher, Mrs. Whiteside, asked her if she had read '*Ann of Green Gables*'.

"She is a young girl in a fiction story written by Lucy Maude Montgomery. Ann dyed her hair green and when I look at you I think of the story." Mrs. Whiteside's own white hair was a hint of blue. *She should talk?*

Chris smiled and chuckled along with her peers when they reacted. With time, it faded away.

*****

Eddy left because there had been a major confrontation between him and Mr. Kirk, the school principal. Mr. Kirk grabbed hold of Eddy's brother, Ric, and threatened to cut off his pompadour hair, always falling over Ric's eyes. Dress code and personal appearance was always enforced. Girls could not wear slacks or jeans. Boys were not allowed blue jeans or cleats on their shoes. Hair, of much length, was not tolerated on boys. Eddy, enraged with the principal for getting after Ric, lipped him off. He was disrespectful with other teacher before. One of them carried him, by his ears, to the office. Eddy faced suspension.

CHAPTER 36

Chris carried on with the same group of friends after Eddy left. This group often hung out at Eddy's and Ric's home. Their parent's, Ann and Al welcomed the gang at any time, all the time. Whenever Chris went over there, she was always eager for news about Eddy. The feeling in their family home was welcoming. She felt free to ask and speak without getting told off. Ann was called *Mom* by all the young people, and she seemed to enjoy the company of the youths who often turned to her for a sympathetic ear.

Ann offered encouragement and always laughed at the stories they told. Al worked in oil-patch construction and was away for weeks at a time.

Chris' parents discouraged all but one girl friend at a time to visit Chris at home. Never would they allow a group of mixed teens over to play cards or listen to records or watch TV. She accepted their rule and never hoped it to change for fear her mum would be in a cranky mood and not think twice about embarrassing her in front of her friends.

Eddy was away and thoughts of him were pushed to the back of Chris' mind. Her time was busy, filled with helping out plenty at home, babysitting elsewhere for spending money, and keeping up with homework, and all else which came with school life. Chris enjoyed this particular time the most of any time since coming to Canada. She found peace at home by being diligent, swift and efficient at household chores, without being told and she never complained about it.

Adept at arranging her mother's hair, Chris felt as though she mastered her mother's approval through her usefulness. Ava seemed proud of her, at this time too, because Chris was crowned *Acadia Teen Queen*, a title she won by selling the most raffle tickets and judged on a talent. She recited a poem.

Her parents were pleased with her report card. *What more could they want?* Chris could not understand why high marks mattered to them other than they were able to comment about how good they were and that was maybe how they rated their success of parenting. The benefit of success in education for Chris herself was never discussed at home—not what career or opportunities lay ahead for the young girl other than Ava assumed she would be a hairstylist, marry well, have children and most important, keep a spotless house and present delicious meals.

After just arriving home from school, Chris heard, "Dere is a letter from Bedstemor if you vaunt to read it," Ava remarked. Chris rushed for the letter, hungry for news from Denmark. The letter contained news of the death of Mrs. Kjaer. Chris associated the name right away with the name she knew to be the same surname as her real father. Many times she snooped through papers in her mother's dresser drawer, searching for proof of her own identity because no one ever volunteered to discuss the subject. She was afraid to bring up a 'not to talk about' subject, still, she determined to explore right then and there.

Something strong within her drove out the words, "Who is Mrs. Kjaer?"

"Oh, just an old lady friend of Bedstemor," Ava sloughed it off.

With a huge rush of adrenalin, Chris burst out, "Why not tell me the truth? Why not? I know who Mrs. Kjaer was. She was my grandmother! I hate being a secret. I hate it!"

Ava, stunned, retorted "How do you know? Who told?"

"For God's sake, I was at your wedding. I remember when you got married to Erling. I know! I just know!"

"Hush up, right now, do you hear me? Dad is in the shower. He vil be mad if he hears you. Never talk about dis again. He has been good to you. You vil make him feel bad, enough! No more to be said!"

Chris retreated downstairs to her room with tears of anguish on the verge of spilling over. She did not want Erling's anger nor did she want him to feel hurt but what about her pain? She fought with her heartbreak once again.

CHAPTER 37

Chris met a boy by the name of Jim. He reminded her just a little of Eddy. He was polite and Chris enjoyed spending time with him. Jim visited a few times wherever she babysat and they enjoyed cuddling close and sharing a few kisses. They danced well together and attended a dance program taped for television broadcast at a local Calgary TV station.

Jim broached the subject of Chris' crush on Eddy, and hinted at how he expected to be dumped if Eddy showed up, back on the scene. Chris brushed off the subject not knowing how to answer.

One Saturday afternoon, at Teen and Twenty, Eddy showed up with the rest of the usual gang and when it was time to leave, Eddy invited Chris and Jim to ride back with them instead of taking the bus. Jim guided Chris into the back seat, instead of following her, he turned, said goodbye and headed for the bus. That was the end of Jim and Chris' friendship. It was Easter and Eddy was home to stay.

Teen life went on. Chris felt happy whenever she was able to escape from home. She exaggerated and outright lied to her parents to gain permission to attend both real and fictional functions. It was a challenge to get her parents to bend on her curfew. They would not bend. It was eleven o'clock p.m. or nothing. Being at the dance for the last dance and then getting to go with the gang to the A&W Drive-in meant an awful lot to her. She came home as expected, pretended to go to bed and then snuck out the laundry room window. After all the others in their group had to go home, she and Eddy parked with and found plenty of opportunity to grow fonder and deeper in their relationship.

Ava gave Chris permission to skip school one day to be a spectator at the High School Track Competition, Ava believed in sports. The truth was Chris spent the day at Eddy's house. He dropped out of school and was taking his welding apprenticeship, working shift work. The two young lovers got together during the day or not much at all. A teacher at school decided to give Ava a call exploring whether or not she knew of Chris' absenteeism. A huge misunderstanding followed.

"I know my daughter missed school. It vas important, don't bodder me again!" Ava told the teacher off without proper understanding of how frequent Chris was absent. A communication barrier due to poor English saved Chris, this time.

Forgery was easy for Chris, without a feeling of guilt because Ava asked her to pretend to be Ava when the creditors called. She instructed Chris to get rid of them by saying her husband would be in with the money soon. It seemed the couple spent far more than their budget allowed. Buying a new house was just the beginning. There were all the things to go in it and outside it.

The first time Chris became an impostor without permission was in order to protect her brother, Karl. Answering the phone, hearing an adult voice Chris prepared to spiel off the usual to a creditor or bank manager. But, it was the owner of the neighborhood *Tom Boy* store, reporting Karl was caught shop lifting a carton of cigarettes. Chris made her decision and carried on, "Yes, yes, this is his mother all right! I cannot believe my son would do that. I appreciate your concern and understand something has to be done, and, I appreciate you will let us deal with him in this matter. You can be sure he will not shoplift again. Thank you for calling." Chris could not bear to see or hear the younger ones getting hit and yelled at. Her stomach tied up in knots and her head pounded, *what was she to do?*

Karl came through the door, prepared for his mother's wrath, He was in the store keepers office when the call was made home. Chris stood at the top of the stairs when Karl came in, watching him cowering, "Where's Mum? How mad is she?"

"Mum? She is sleeping, hush up and go outside. I'll be talking to you."

In the front yard they talked. Karl got as good a lecture as Chris could deliver with a warning he better behave and not let it happen again.

CHAPTER 38

One day, Erling needed another driver to deliver a car to the other side of Calgary. Ava didn't have a license nor did under age Chris, but she had the guts to try if Erling was willing to let her, "Follow me right behind," instructed Erling. Chris had no problem at all and Erling praised her for being a natural born driver.

"Wow, Chris!" said Diane, when Chris pulled up in front of her best friend's house, in Erling's car, with Karl sitting beside her, "are you nuts—out of your head—taking your dad's car?"

"My Dad said I could come over here but that's all. It's just two long blocks, no big deal." Chris insisted. After chatting awhile Chris suggested Diane come for a little spin with her.

"Back, to your house?"

"Let's go a little bit further, like to Ed's house," Chris whispered, "we'll be back here, soon. My dad will never know."

Chris maneuvered the 1959 push button automatic orange and white Dodge through the streets, a little nervous, "egad, the streets seem narrower here don't you think?" No sooner said when a scraping sound was heard.

"What was that?" exclaimed Diane.

"Oh, you silly, nothing much, it was just a rock in the road." Chris tried to sound sure of her-self.

"I think you hit a parked car," Diane continued.

Karl spouted, "I'm telling, I'm telling."

Chris headed for home but stopped before all the way there to inspect. Not one single mark on dad's car, thank goodness. "All right now do you believe me? And you Karl, you don't even breathe anything about this at all because I have a story to tell about cigarette thieving."

The near ten year old Karl, kept quiet but not without teasing and tormenting when he wanted something from Chris. It worked both ways.

CHAPTER 39

After a couple of years in Canada, Chris was promised a trip back to Denmark to summer with the relatives there, as she did before. First it was, "It'll have to be next summer ven vee have more money." Then it was, "We bought the house dis year , it vil have to be next summer."

Other Danish immigrant children they were acquainted with went. Chris felt angry inside and anguished at losing touch with everyone back home. *How could her parents do this to her?*

She realized it would not happen. By the time the next spring rolled around and Erling informed her all charter flights were full. Chris had a much bigger worry on her mind.

She went all the way a couple of times with Eddy and last month her period was late a week. She was relieved when it came. After swearing never to do it again, she did. Now, again, she was worried about her time of the month coming. *Please, please I can't be pregnant. I will get killed. Eddy said it would be okay.*

"Pulling out in time, works. You won't get pregnant, don't worry."

Chris worried and for good reason. She was late, one week, two weeks, a month, six weeks and then a visit to the doctor. Eddy went to *People's Credit Jewelers* and bought a set of wedding rings the night before the appointment. On bended knee, he asked Chris to marry him.

"We are too young. If I'm pregnant I'll have the baby and we'll get married later. I don't want you to marry me because I'm pregnant."

"If you are not pregnant let's still get engaged, please Chris."

144

Chris acted, to give him a chance to get out of it. She was just testing him, hoping all along he still would want to marry her and love her for the rest of his life. She had no trouble at all visualizing, fantasizing about the perfect marriage and children they would have together. Chris did not feel too young or incapable of being a wife and a mother if she had to be.

At the doctor's office Chris evaded the crux of the matter as if avoiding the truth would make her un-pregnant. "What are you here for young lady?"

"Oh, I haven't been feeling quite right . . . I'm not sure."

"Is there a chance you are pregnant?" The doctor forced Chris into facing reality.

"A small chance, maybe, but, please, I hope not," she said, as if she were trying to get him to enter into the denial with her.

The doctor's voice sounded hollow, echoing over the wire as if from a vacuum filled space, "The test is positive. You are pregnant." Chris let the receiver clatter back in position on its cradle, and stared at the phone as if it were an enemy. In her head was the aftermath of his first few words, not registering quite clear, but something about her parents and then regular check-ups? With limbs feeling like half-set jelly, the stricken girl put head in hands while the tears flowed. Ed standing by, watching and waiting put his arms around her. He cuddled her in silence, for a long time. Afterwards they began planning their next move.

"We will have to tell our parents right away. We can start planning a wedding," Ed took charge.

"No, I must wait, I need to think, rehearse the words. My Mum is in the hospital for surgery. We have to wait till she comes home."

"No Chris, not that long."

"Just let's have the weekend then before we tell? We will go to the drive-in. Please, let us wait, I'm scared. I might get sent away. I'll never see you again?"

"Okay Chris."

Eddy brought Chris home later the same afternoon. He came in with her, just for a while he said. Erling just got home from work and Chris knew supper must be fixed, right away. Erling, acting polite, greeted Eddy, which surprised Chris. It was helpful, her mother was absent from the home, unable to make them feel uncomfortable, thought Chris.

Only once before, had Eddy been there. Chris persuaded her mother to allow a mixed sixteenth birthday party—it only lasted a couple of hours. Ava was accepting and made the little Danish pancake balls called aebleskiver. The fellows enjoyed the eating contest of how many they could eat and they were generous with compliments for Ava about her wonderful treat. Chris thought the afternoon went better than she could have ever hoped for. Whenever Eddy came too close to Chris she made sure to back off right away and once when he succeeded in putting his arms around her a quick shove set him in retreat, puzzled. Chris glanced over her shoulder, praying Mum didn't notice—she knew she'd catch hell later.

This day without Ava at home it seemed easier for Chris. She was surprised when she heard Erling ask, "Are you eating supper vit us tonight, Ed?"

"Gee, thanks, I would like to."

In the kitchen, Chris carried on with preparations for a simple supper for three. Since Ava was in the hospital, the younger children were staying elsewhere. The TV was on in the living room, there was no conversation until Ed broke the silence, "I ah….I need to speak with you sir….in private….Please?"

Chris stopped stirring the gravy, hung on to the counter, and thought about running out the back door. She was betrayed—Ed broke their agreement.

"Best come vit me den," Erling demanded as he rose from his easy chair and led the way to the master bedroom.

In automated stupor the shocked girl carried on with the meal preparation anticipating the worst. There were no loud voices, nor any sound of physical attack. She heard the bedroom door open. Next she heard their footsteps coming toward the kitchen. Chris kept her back turned, fighting for composure, and strength to look Erling square in the eyes.

Erling opened the fridge door, reached inside, "I need a beer, how about you, Ed?"

"Well, ah….no ah….well okay sure," Ed's voice, weaker than normal replied.

A beer offering— Chris interpreted this as a good thing but she darn near keeled over when Erling gestured to her as if she may want one too. A shake of her head "no" was all she replied.

In awkward silence, the three began the simple meal. Erling laid down his cutlery after his last mouthful, placed his large hands on the table and tapped his fingers, "I vil tell your modder in a few days. Ed here, says you vaunt to marry but what about you Chris? Are you ready for dat? Tink about it and vee vil vait until your modder comes home for more talk."

Sleep came easy that night, compared to the struggle of the past few nights. Chris knew facing her mother would not be as calm a situation as it was with Erling. She was grateful Erling offered to tell Ava. *Oh no, who will tell Bedstemor and what will she and Bedstefar think of me?*

*****

Ed decided to inform his parents by himself— easiest was telling his dad. Al was on a job in Fort McMurray, "Do you need me, to come home?" He asked Ed, "Just remember you don't have to get married. You don't have to do anything you don't want to do."

Ann, however, struggled, tried to find a solution, flipped back and forth between kindness and meanness toward Chris.

"Ed, you are much too young, you and Chris both. I say you wait to get married much later, wait until you are sure you want to marry. You are too young to know what you want. I will raise the baby the first few years to help out until you two are more mature."

"No, mom, I want to marry Chris and she will never give the baby up to anyone. We have already talked about all the things we might do and our minds are made up."

"Ed, you are being ridiculous! How do you know it's your baby? It might not be! Has she never, ever, dated anybody else? Think about it Ed!—Did she trap you—a trick to get away from her parents? You could be ruining your whole life!"

"Mom, help us or don't, accept or not, we will get married somehow!"

With hurt and anger, Ed left his mother alone to deal with her hysterics. He felt burdened with the huge responsibility ahead, and disappointed and disgusted at his mother's outburst of irrational grasping at trying to secure his freedom.

Ed drove about without direction, alone....Hours passed. Ann calmed down, started to worry about Ed, phoned around, and asked about him. A friend, Jim offered to look for him and found Ed's car parked at Fish Creek. Ed was wading, sloshing around, weaving as if drunk, but he was not drunk—he was sick—he was crying. Jim calmed him, helped him snap back to reality and instructed him to follow to Jim's house.

Jim and his wife, Flo, friends and chaperones through their teen club, intervened, speaking for Ed with Ann. When Ann realized the condition of her son, she changed her attitude and began to support the inevitable upcoming marriage. Ed's stress caused temporary paralysis to half of his face.

*****

With her lips squeezed together tight, no natural lip color showed, Ava aimed her dagger eyes at Chris, who came up the five steps from the landing. Chris halted at the railing and held on.

"I hear you are growing a big belly. Didn't I tell you enough, many times? I told you, guys only vaunt de one ting but you didn't learn your lesson from vat I told you. Well, you vil find out. Life is no picnic, no bed of roses. You've made your bed, now lie in it—remember, don't come running home ven tings don't work out. We got enough mouts to feed! How many times did you do it?"

Chris cringed inside at the tongue lashing and answered with, "only once," as if it would cool her mother's temper. Chris resented the prying and wanted to hang on to her privacy of the intimacy she shared with Ed. The two of them shared love and caring, not the sordid picture Ava implied.

*****

For a few days following Ava's homecoming, there was no wedding plan talk at all.

Ava gave one of her oppressive silence treatments with sighing and door slamming. Ava appeared to be in deep dark thought. Ava announced her solution to Chris' pregnancy, "I've talked to a doctor and you are having an abortion."

"I am not. I don't care what you want—you can't make me—I will run away, far away, away from you. You are hateful, mean—you don't love anybody—not your husband--not your kids—only yourself! I'm surprised you didn't abort all your kids. I know you had an abortion, which I never will have and I will love my baby more than you ever could. My baby will never feel unwanted like I always feel!" Chris' voice, loud and accusing, threw Ava into a maniacal rage. Kicking, punching, pushing, she attacked Chris.

"You whore, you're dirty, shame on you, I hate you for de trouble you are! Get out, get out, you little whore!" Ava pushing and pushing had Chris backing up, near the stairs. Tripping, tumbling, down the five steps to the landing, Chris lay prone protecting herself with her arms held up. Ava still pursued her, slapping shoving, screaming, kicking until Chris rolled down the second set of five stairs, managed to get up and head towards her own room with Ava right behind. She gave her one last shove into the room. Ava grabbed the door handle and slammed the door. She marched upstairs still yelling obscenities. Stunned, shocked, and heartbroken Chris shivered in anguish. She heard her mother yelling into the phone. "Come and get your hoore out of my house—you made her pregnant you take care of her," followed by the receiver, slamming down hard.

Ed came as fast as he could, worried for Chris' welfare. Ava scared him with her screeching and obscenities. He entered the house, went straight to Chris' room, "Come on, hurry let's get out of here, your mother is off her rocker." Chris allowed herself to be led out of the house, into Ed's car, and then into his house, his mother was not at home. He tucked Chris into his bed by herself. She was freezing, sobbing, and making no sense at all. Ed calmed Chris down and went to sit and think about things in the front room. A short while later Erling pulled up in front of the house.

"Vere is Chris and vat's de big idea taking her avay? She is supposed to be at home helping clean de house vit her modder. Vat in hell is going on?" Chris heard Erling bellowing and scrambled out of Ed's bed terrified he should think they had been making love. She was now determined to protect Ed and pulled herself together.

"I'm right here and okay I will come with you but, you must please listen to what I need to say."

"Your modder called me at vork and she has already told me you got hysterical and yelled at her and dat you refused to do any more work around de house," he was loud and stern of voice but he did listen to Chris as she, heartbroken and weeping, got out the truth.

Erling must have believed her. Softly, he said, "get in de car, vee are going home."

Chris entered the house and went straight for the vacuum cleaner but she trembled and the damned up tears overflowed. Her breathing came in gasps and she thought she was going to collapse. Erling came toward her, took the vacuum hose from her hands and mumbled, "Go to your room, take it easy."

Muffled voices filtered down into her room, into her stupor. They were loud, easy to hear, "Ava I don't give a damn how mad you are, you can't treat her like dat. If dat is how you are going to behave den Chris better not live here until dey have a vedding—a vedding is what they . I tink we can't talk dem out of it. You can't force an abortion on Chris." Ava was silenced. Erling went downstairs, knocked on the door and opened it. He pulled up a chair beside Chris' bed and cleared his throat, "Chris vould you like to go live at Ben and Elma's until vee can get you married off. I vil phone, explain, and ask dem?"

"No....No, I will stay right here until my wedding."

*****

Afterwards, Erling went for a meeting with Ann. The two of them shared harsh words, hurling blame in each other's direction. Erling claimed Ed was spoiled with too many privileges and wasn't taught responsibility about sex. Ann claimed Chris became pregnant on purpose to get away from her parents. It was a tense situation but it calmed down.

*****

Ed and Chris chose to see the United Church minister in their neighborhood rather than go to the Danish Lutheran Church, "I will feel more comfortable with your denomination, even if you haven't been to church for a long time. I won't feel as judged," Chris confessed.

"I used to sing in the choir, and attended the youth group meetings until just before we moved to Calgary. My mother got mad at our minister and put a stop to us going," Ed replied.

After one visit with the Minister and answering his questions, he agreed to perform the ceremony. "Good that's done, he was kind without lecturing us about being too young," Chris said with relief in her voice.

"For sure, I liked him too. Now we have to go through the dreaded Marriage License affair with four parents in tow to sign the consent form," Ed said.

"Oh, don't remind me, I hope we can meet them there. I can't do an outing with my Mum yakking at me there and back. The blood test was less painful , I'm sure."

Ed drove his parent's car to the Vital Statistics Office.

"I don't agree vit dis, ja, but I have to sign don't I?" Ava whined. Chris held her breath and watched for problems. The clerk didn't flinch, maybe Ava's broken English went by the wayside. After the signing, and stamping of the document the clerk announced, "That will be twenty five dollars please." Heads turned towards Ed while he groped and patted in search for his wallet.

"Gees, I forgot my wallet, sorry. Mom, Dad, can you help?" Ed asked.

"No, Ed, here. I made the money when I babysat for Mum's co-worker in July. You owe me though," Chris said with a giggle. Everyone laughed.

"Okay my son," Al chided, "no wallet, no driver's license, you get the back seat home."

. Al, the pragmatic one of Chris' in-laws, offered Ed a flight ticket, to anywhere Ed might desire, to hide, to get out of his predicament on the day before the wedding. Chris felt no anger towards Al, just pure and simple joy— Ed stuck by her no matter what!

The church wedding took place even though Ava insisted they should be going to the justice of the peace because Chris, pregnant and all, did not deserve a wedding in church and dressed in white.

Thanks to Aunt Elma's hand-me down wedding gown, Chris had her church wedding in white and a reception was held at the Beacon Hotel in Calgary on August 28th, 1965.

The guests consisted of close relatives from both sides, none came from Denmark. Members from the teen club came, and also from a Danish group Ava and Erling belonged to. Alcohol was served, but Ed and Chris requested milk for themselves at the head table, and the rest of the evening.

CHAPTER 40

Wendy stood crying, on the sidewalk, waving her outstretched arms, upset to see her older sister driving away with Ed after packing up a few boxes. Chris experienced a bitter sweet emotion— saddened to leave her much loved siblings—who would protect them from the wrath of their mother now?—Yes, she admitted to Ed she felt guilty about it but, oh, how happy, and what a relief it was to escape all the tensions of living with them.

Ava's parting words of wisdom, "You remember vat I say—life is not a bed of roses."

Chris did not reply. She showed her disapproval of the statement with a copy of an expression she had seen on her mother's face too many times. *I vow I will with all my might do everything I can to make a bed of roses and I will endeavor to be loving and funny like Bedstemor, who is the opposite in character to my Mother.*

*****

Chris moved just five blocks away from Archwood Road to Alcott Road. But, what a different atmosphere it was! This was temporary, of course, they all agreed. The young couple was too poor to have their own place right away.

Ed's mother, Ann, warmed in acceptance of their marriage. Ed's father, Al, also accepted Ed's decision. Al was absent for long periods of time—away at work—in Fort McMurray, the Alberta Tar Sands.

"Chris, pick out the material from these bolts of cloth for the new curtains for your bedroom. I will have them sewn up in a jiffy," Ann directed Chris in planning the redecorating of the bedroom Ed and she occupied, in the house. At the same time, the whole house got painted.

Ann went to work part time at Woodward's delicatessen and Chris enjoyed the position of chief housekeeper and cook for the household, consisting of seven full time residents. Besides the newlyweds and Ann, there was Ed's younger brother, Ric, and a foster brother, Billy, who is a native Indian placed in foster care by social services. He still attended school but hoped to escape the situation and find work. Jim and Wayne also lived there, paying for room and board, while working at Dominion Bridge, the same place as Ed works. The arrangement was Ed and Chris live there in exchange for Chris' household labor, laundry, cleaning, cooking, daily lunches and so on. Grocery moneys came from the boarders and the rest of household expenses were paid by Ann and Al.

The household hummed with activity most of the time. Teen friends came in and out, as always, early or late. Chris learned how to use a wringer washing machine––it was a tough lesson. *I must stay alert. I sure don't want my hand going through the wringer again.* She had stood in horror, watching, as her hand followed the pillow case in-between the rollers. With confusion and uncertainty she finally turned the dial. The rollers changed direction and she observed her hand roll back out. Chris ran around the basement screeching, crying with the pain. Jim and Wayne thundered down the stairs, at the distressing sound of the wailing. They thought Chris must be having a baby already.

*****

"Chris put some meat on those sandwiches," Ann admonished, "Ed will starve!"

Chris marveled at the thickly filled sandwiches as Ann took charge and demonstrated what she meant by a proper sandwich.

"We eat well here, so much good food. Ann, you're a wonderful cook and I hope you will teach me more." She taught Chris and introduced her to all the wonderful Ukrainian recipes.

Ann brought home cold cuts, cheeses, breads and salads from the Deli. Chris ate with more abandonment than she had ever known and had a rapid weight gain during her pregnancy. The doctor stated his concern and Chris shared this with Ann.

"OH, to heck with him! You're eating for two. When I had Betty Ann I gained forty pounds and overnight lost forty pounds." Ann loved everyone to eat a lot at her house.

She and Chris baked together and enjoyed the whole social aspect of it from beginning to consumption.

*****

Visits to Chris' parent's home were made out of a sense of duty. Chris felt nervous each time. She had no hope at all for harmony between herself and her Mother. *She does not want me to be happy. She does not have to say it. I feel it.*

Often, Ava responded to her daughter's comments with sarcasm and *'telling you so stories'* for preparing her for delivery. "Ja, ven I had you, it was forty eight hours of horrible pain. You came out all blue, and thought to be dead, but no, you lived. Your Oldemor, vorried you might have brain damage. You'll be sorry, ven your turn comes, just wait and see."

Chris vowed no matter what was in store for her, how bad or good, it would be something not to talk about, with her Mum. She felt her mother wanted to punish her—destroy her happiness, she wondered why? *Does anyone else sense how it is between us or is she cunning enough to inflict this truth on me alone?*

*****

It appeared Ava came to like Ed,teasing around him in a flirtatious manner. Ed took it all in and went along in his happy, lighthearted way that came so natural to him. Always affectionate, he delighted in cuddling Chris and kissing her wherever and whenever the thought occurred to him. Chris basked in his adoration and returns his affection except in the presence of her parents. There she cringed, stiffened, and withdrew. Afterwards, when alone, they would argue. Ed demanded to know what is bugging her.

"Ed don't you see their looks, striking us apart as if a hatchet chopping through a piece of wood? Don't hug, kiss, or tell me you love me in front of my parents, please? You just don't understand! You don't know them! It's different in your family! You are lucky!"

CHAPTER 41

In the seventh month of pregnancy, Ed and Chris recognized the need for privacy and for the chance to set up housekeeping alone together. Not any one big disaster happened in the arrangement just a lot of little things, plaguing Chris, more than Ed. She found it overwhelming— so many people coming and going much of the time. She felt tired, overcome with her duties and worried about being judged as a lazy person. She had a great need to prove herself worthy and capable of all she thought everyone expected of her.

When Ed's pay was raised from ninety eight cents an hour, as a first year apprentice welder, to one dollar and twenty five cents an hour, the young couple rejoiced.

"Let's look for a place of our own!" said Ed as he reached out for his wife and kissed her swollen belly.

Earlier they managed to buy a used Corvair. Transportation was not a problem any longer. They loved searching for a place. After seeing hopeless filthy, old, run down places and expensive decent ones, luck was with them when they discovered an old war time house near downtown Calgary. The owners, busy with redecorating after kicking out bad tenants eyed them with disbelief, Chris thought probably because of their young age and her obvious pregnancy.

They talked a blue streak trying to impress the landlords, to get them to see them as perfect potential tenants. At seventy dollars a month rent it was a little over the fifty to sixty dollar range they budgeted for. They got the main floor and the unfinished basement of the house. Two single, working girls, lived upstairs. They were proud of their negotiating because neither stove nor refrigerator came with the house but the kind landlords decided to supply them, and even drapes and curtains. A wringer washer, in the basement, came too.

*****

Chris felt tension from Ann and shared it with Ed, "Ed, your mom is mad at us," Chris said with worry in her voice, "she does not want us to move out."

"Oh, she'll get over it," Ed never worried about what others thought. He never fretted or lost sleep. Chris felt sorrowful, and hurt, because Ann would not see their side of it.

As the boarders' payments went to Chris for purchasing groceries—which she had done—she felt rightful in asking for some of the side of beef, bought with the boarders' money for stocking the freezer.

"I only expect a little of it, did I not work for it?" Ann did not agree and Chris dropped the subject and did not take any when they moved.

Chris kept house in pure contentment. Her parent's generosity floored her. For a belated wedding gift they let them pick out a furniture grouping—three rooms of furniture for three hundred dollars. It was not the sturdiest or fanciest but it was new and clean. What a joy, unpacking all their wedding gifts, arranging and re-arranging in their cozy apartment.

Two days before payday, they walked to the corner store, bought a loaf of bread and two chocolate bars. Penniless but happy they snuggled together savoring their sweet contentment.

Ann mellowed after the move, and brought meat when she came for a first visit. She invited them for Sunday dinner, which turned out to be every Sunday dinner. They played a lot of different card games which Chris learned to play and enjoy. The food was always delicious, and plenty of it. Most times there were left overs which Ed and Chris were invited to take home.

*****

"I phoned you but you vere not home, I guess you vere at Ann's?" Ava's tone was pouty, accusatory.

"Ah...yes, we were," Chris anticipated a derogatory reply.

"You always go dere. Don't you know you could come here too? Dat Ed! He vil never let go of his mother's apron strings. He is a mommy's boy. You have a family too, Ja!"

"Oh Mother, don't..." Chris began in self-defense when Ava slammed down the phone. Chris wept. *Never, will I understand her black moods.*

To Ed she said, "She wants and expects us to visit. How can we go there, and feel comfortable in the atmosphere she creates?"

CHAPTER 42

Chris' father-in-law, Al, was due home from Fort McMurray for a week-end visit. The flight ended in Edmonton, where he needed to be picked up. Ed was eager to see his dad and wanted to make the trip. Chris and Ed stayed overnight with Ann on the day before. Ed could make an early start and Chris would have company should she go into labor. She was five days past her due date.

During the night, restlessness overcame her to the point of having to get out of bed, and walk around. Ann, still awake, is reading in her bed. Her door is open and she sees Chris up.

"Chris? Are you all right?"

"Oh....sure....I just can't sleep."

"Are you in any pain at all?"

"No-no, I don't think so."

"Well you know it might be your time, Chris!" Ann sounded nervous.

Chris tried not to think about this time, too afraid to concentrate on the inevitable. *I have not told anyone how scared I really am.* She was determined to be stoic, self-assured. *No-one, at all, will hear me whine about this....No-one!*

"Chris? I am going to wake Ed. I think we should drive you to the hospital, Ann said already half dressed.

"It might be false labor you know? I have heard, it happens lots of times."

"Chris, no, I don't think so!" Ann sounded strict and does not hesitate to get her son out of bed.

They stopped at their own place situated a couple of blocks from The Holy Cross Hospital. The suitcase was picked up and they continued. *I'll imagine my way out of this. Maybe I will faint and wake up when it's over or maybe they will put me to sleep and....Oh God, help me, please?* Chris prayed in silence.

"Yes, you are in labor all right but heck you will be a long time, first baby and you, so young! TCH! TCH! Welcome to the grown up world. I will check in on you once in a while, honey, see you later," the nurse advised, swung her wide hips and vanished out of the institutional green labor room. Ed and Ann walked in.

"Chris, I will try to get somebody else to go get my dad. Do you want me to stay with you?" Ed looked uncomfortable.

"No, of course not....don't be silly....You go....You have to!"

"Are you sure, Chris?"

"Sure, I'm sure*." I wish I had nerve to ask him to stay.*

"Chris I'm sorry but I don't like hospitals," Ann said, "I wouldn't be any good for you here I'm too nervous to stay and keep you company. Do you want me to phone your mother maybe she can come sit with you?"

"Do not, please, don't ask her. Don't phone her. I want to tell her myself when it's over." *No way, do I want her showing up here, smiling, saying, Ja, I told you so. Didn't I?*

Ed gave Chris a big hug and kisses then walked out with his mother in tow.

Chris never yelled out or complained. In silence she begged for someone to please, please come be with her. Chris thought of other times when she fervently wished the same. Abandoned, scared, and with false bravery, she labored. She endured student nurses probing for the size of an orange as the charge nurse instructed them in their search. Chris felt like a science experiment, and wondered if they were referring to her baby's head as an orange. But, Chris remained polite and accommodating.

"Miss or, ah, Mrs.? Do you want me to get the nurse?" questioned a housekeeping staff member who came in to mop the floor.

"I don't know....oh My God....I don't know," Chris grunted out these words while an uncontrollable pushing, bearing down urge, overtook all of her senses and abilities. The rest happened so fast. She give birth to a healthy, seven pounds two ounces, baby girl at 10:30 in the morning. *What a relief from the horrible back pain, like sharp knives stabbing for too long.* She was told her baby came out with head facing up instead of down or vice versa or whatever they said.

"You sure were brave," the nurses commented and Chris beamed at their praise. *I feel like I have done the most important thing in the world, so special. I am proud and happy..*

"Wait, please. I need to make a phone call to my parents,"

The gurney stopped at the nurse's desk on the way to Chris' hospital room. She was offered the use of the phone.

"Hi, Mum....It's me, Chris."

"Oh, hi,"

"I had a baby girl," Chris said in a monotone voice. She was keeping her happiness inside herself.

"Oh? How was dat?" Ava replied in matching monotone.

"It was okay."

"Okay, tanks for phoning. Bye-bye."

Empty, she makes me feel empty. I won't think any more about her today!

Chris' hospital room filled with Ed, his family, friends, flowers and gifts. Happy, happy, all were happy.

Chris felt important, special, as she basked in glory. Everyone shared in the glow associated with the birth of Kari Lynn, February 19th, 1966.

CHAPTER 43

Taking care of her daughter was easy for Chris. With her background as frequent care giver to her younger siblings, she accepted motherhood without any qualms for someone of her age. She made many trips to the crib side, listening for her baby's breathing. Sometimes she woke with a start, afraid she may have fallen asleep while nursing Kari in their bed. She worried she or Ed might roll on top of the baby, and end up smothering her.

The day Ava called to say she was catching the bus, and coming for a visit on her day off from work, sent Chris into a cleaning frenzy. *I have to show her perfection, not one sign of not coping, no siree! Make-up, hair-do, all.. God Almighty what will I wear?*
None of Chris' clothing from before the pregnancy fit her. Ann's prediction of 'it'll come off, overnight,' did not come true, far from it. Of the forty pound gain, Chris lost a total of ten pounds giving birth. Part of Ed's next paycheck would buy clothes for Chris. She put on a clean house-coat and greeted Ava at the door.

"Hi, did I get you out of bed?" enquired Ava.

"No, Mother, my clothes are in the laundry. I plan to do it later, please come in, its cold."

"Hang up my coat and here's a package."

"Oh, gee, you didn't have to bring a present, thank you."

"Ha, vait till you see first. It's more for Ed, you tell him to use dem. He von't like dem but make him anyway. Vee doesn't need dem anymore since dat surgery."

Chris' face flushed with embarrassment, anger too. She uttered nary a word. She set the offensive hand-me-down, left over condoms, aside.

Ava did fuss and coo over Kari and asked about christening plans, "Vee have to have de dress sent over you know."

"Yes, thank you I will like it a lot, Mum, go ahead."

Ava put on the Christening dinner and enjoyed telling the story of the gown, "Ja, I vas first. My Grandmodder made it for me. I am oldest of five girls. It is forty one years old and all my sisters' kids have been in it too. Ja, all of mine too. Chris was in it. Vee changes to new ribbon for each baby—blue for boys and pink for girls."

Chris felt proud of this bit of history. She knew her Mum did too and for that short interval—their minds and hearts were a little connected.

This was another one of those times when Chris' mind would flit back to Denmark and the relatives and think 'if only thoughts'. Guest numbers for the Christening was small. In Denmark it would be much larger, fancier too. Canadian custom doesn't seem to put much priority on fancy. Ava did make the table formal, decorated Danish style, using a pink color theme. During dinner, Kari had a nap on her grandmother's bed. She woke and began to cry. In an instant, Chris pushed back her chair.

"Sit down, you stay here, finish eating!" Erling commanded with stern authority in his voice. Chris hesitated for a short moment. Without a word, she glanced back at him, and went to her baby.

CHAPTER 44

Chris' parents took Canadian Citizenship for themselves and Karl but not for her. It didn't seem right to Chris.

"I married in this country and I have a baby here, and I'm a Danish citizen. I feel a strong need. I must be a Canadian citizen with a sense of belonging. I don't see myself returning to Denmark now. Ed, we must be the same." Ed agreed and helped her with the questions she would be tested on.

Chris became a Canadian citizen. She knew the names of all the provinces, their capital cities, and she knew the name of the Prime Minister. She swore allegiance to Canada and the Queen. Just like her marriage license this Certificate was in her legal name of Kirsten Marie. She applied for her social insurance card as Mrs. E. unsure of the name she wanted on the card.

CHAPTER 45

Chris was distraught and said, "Ed, we must move. We don't have a choice!"

"Yes, Chris, we must...." They knew they had to give up their little doll house. They couldn't afford the rent while Ed attended SAIT for six weeks. The unemployment pay he was entitled to was not going to be enough. They couldn't borrow the money because they couldn't afford to pay it back later.

"Our solution is to take Ann and Al's offer of free rent, living back at their house. They are making a trip to the States and your brother Ric is travelling with them during summer break from school. We will take care of the house. Billy still lives there but no one else, the work is minimal," Chris was positive this was the right thing to do. She convinced Ed.

Ed passed his first year with high marks, "Thanks honey, without your help with my studying, I don't think I would have done this well. You could pass the exam too."

"Maybe the written test, but a practical test—I would have a big problem, welding."

When they could afford it, they looked for another doll house but no luck this time. The best they found in their price range was a basement suite with tiny windows and cold linoleum floors. They made the best of it....for a little while.

The owners lived upstairs. The man, an Italian brick layer was home a lot. His wife, a school teacher, maintained regular work hours and their two daughters were both in elementary school. At first they seemed kind and acted as friends would. But, Chris became uncomfortable in the man's presence, the way he looked at her, for a start and then his comments.

"Ah.... you are a Danish girl....you lucky boy, Ed! What's it like to have your own little sex kitten? Eh boy? The way I read in the porno rags, all those Scandinavian girls practice free love. Nudity all over the place and Christ's sake—none of them, makes it past twelve as a virgin. They do it with cousins, even brothers! You're a lucky, son of a bitch!"

"Oh, he's just teasing!" interjected his wife. She threw her husband a murderous look.

Ed and Chris sat dumbfounded, red faced, speechless. After their visit Chris told Ed how embarrassed she was, "why does anyone have the right to say such a thing? I come from strictness itself!"

"Honey, I don't know. I should have slapped his face but I was stunned. I'm sorry for you I didn't. Don't pay any attention to it."

*****

"Hello....the milkman is here!" Fear gripped Chris, surprise and anger too,

"I thought my door was locked. Don't bring my milk in again. I prefer to do it myself." Chris took the milk from the landlord and breathed a sigh of relief when he went back out. Another day when Chris was doing the laundry, he came down to the shared facility on a pretense

170

and made small talk about the drying conditions of the weather. Chris made her way up the stairs with the basket of clothes to hang up. He followed close behind her and pinched her bottom.

"Don't ever, do that again!" Chris tried to sound angry. She was sure it sounded too timid because she was shaking, nervous and scared.

Time passed without anything but a polite hello from their Italian landlord. Chris started to feel more at ease. He went to work a lot more than when first they moved in. His wife didn't have much time for chatting. She was always polite whenever Chris met her around the premises. Their two young daughters came to see baby Kari and stayed awhile to entertain her whenever they had the chance.

Chris would realize she was living with a false sense of security, "Hello?" Chris answered the phone mid-morning.

"Hi, How are you doing down there?" Dread crept over Chris, she held her breath awhile. "Hey, it's me, your landlord, calling to invite you upstairs for lunch today!"

"Ah, what, No—no, I think not."

"Oh, come on, I just want to be friends."

"Who else will be there? Is your wife coming home for lunch?"

"Well, of course, she is. She sure wants you to come!"

"Well, okay then, thank you." When Chris heard the little girls come home for lunch as usual, she went upstairs with confidence. The table was decorated with flowers, even wine glasses. "We always have a glass of wine with spaghetti, according to Italian tradition," said the burly landlord.

"Is someone celebrating a birthday?" Chris asked.

"No, it's just an ordinary good neighbor lunch," he dished up the girls right away. "We will wait a bit," he explained as he poured wine.

Chris assumed he meant wait for his wife. The little girls ate in a hurry and wanted to rush off to play with their friends before afternoon classes started. *Something is not feeling right.* Chris began to worry.

"When will your wife be home and does she have the afternoon off? She won't have time to eat if she has to get back to school for afternoon classes, will she?"

"Oh, don't worry. Just have a glass of wine while we wait. She will be here."

"No, thanks. I can't stay I just remembered something I have to do." Chris watched his face get angry, he protested. Chris had to get away. She scooped Kari up, headed for the doorway. He tried persuading her to stay.

"NO! Get out of my way!"

He appeared hurt, pouty. Chris couldn't have cared less. She shook as she hurried downstairs, opened their apartment door, closed it, and turned the lock. Chris put a chair up against it, for extra insurance. *I know the monster has a key.* When Ed came home from work Chris told him right away.

"Maybe it's nothing, maybe it was okay?"

"NO! He's lecherous— you have to help me deal with him!"

172

Ed felt unsure but upstairs he went and returned a few minutes later, angry, "We are moving out, pack up and tomorrow after work I'll get Jim to come help us. We will go back to my folks."

"What happened up there? Did you tell him we are leaving?"

"No, he doesn't know yet and we are not giving notice. He's a jerk—you are right about him. He told me I would have to tell my wife to be nice to him if we wanted to keep this place to live. I told him to go to hell and I left."

Mr. Landlord had one more act to follow. He refused to move his big work truck out of the driveway. They could not back in to load their stuff. He proceeded to hose out the box on his truck, and with malicious intent he splashed the guys and the furnishings as they carried them out to the street. Ed went for the phone, called the police and asked for assistance.

"Chris, don't say a word to the crazy bastard just get on with it. Ignore him the best you can," Ed took charge and waited for the police officer who came and stood by until they finished.

This man wanted 'the one thing,' for sure but I can't share this with my mother. Instead, Chris explained the darkness of a basement suite was unbearable, not exactly an untruth. The young couple moved back to Ed's parent's home.

"Ja, now you are boat tied to Ann's apron strings. I told you, life is not a bed of roses. You are too young. You can't manage without Ed's Mommy and Daddy," Ava flung her words at Chris. She decided not to retaliate even though she had a lot built up inside begging for relief.

Once, a radio talk show's topic centered on adopting away babies and the trauma to a birth mother afterwards. After listening awhile, Chris grabbed the phone as if it was her weapon, surprised to get right through. Her voice stumbled at first then grew strong and confident enabling her to state her opinion.

"I am a child, born out of wedlock, unwanted, and raised by a bitter, cold hearted woman who has had no qualms, in the past, about letting me know the burden she bore. I wish I had been adopted out."

"Audience this is interesting. We have here another side to the story. Go on please and explain further," said the radio host.

"It's not what the child can do for you! I am a mother myself at sixteen, and married. I will be opposite to my Mother. I will do for my child how I wished it was done for me. And, if you can't raise a child with an unselfish attitude then for God's sake, give it up."

Chris got off the phone feeling like she had done a good thing—relieved herself.

CHAPTER 46

The boom at Fort McMurray beckoned to Ed. His Father encouraged him to take adage of this time and opportunity, "Make lots of money, son. Get ahead."

Ed was finding his job at Dominion Bridge stifling, and repetitious, "Chris, we could sure use the money, maybe buy our own house. I need to build on my experience in my trade. I can't see myself stuck in the same shop for long."

"Oh honey, I miss you already, I can't imagine you will get home as little as your Dad does. Maybe we could move to Edmonton, to be nearer each other."

"Well the men do get one day off on Sundays but like Dad says the distance and the road conditions are challenging and most of them stay in camp and rest. But I'm one of the young horny ones. I'd make it home to you one day a week," he comforted Chris with a tight hug and a deep kiss.

*****

There were long tedious hours in a week and much boredom. Chris and baby Kari existed this way for months. A short walk to the bank and across the street for groceries was the most necessary outings in her routine.

One morning she got up and found the contents of the kitchen drawers on top of the counter. Puzzled and alarmed she searched her brain. *What happened here, did someone break in?* Chris had flashbacks back and saw she was doing this. *What is the matter with me?* She pushed it aside and forgot about it but a few nights later she woke up outside the apartment building in her night gown. Frightened she rushed inside relieved no-one was about. Chris knew she was in emotional trouble when she wet her bed. She asked a neighbor for a referral to a doctor then asked her to watch Kari.

Her body was jumpy, her tongue shaky as she explained the upsetting events to the doctor.

"Dear young, lady! I say you are suffering from cabin fever, a real condition, caused by too much isolation. I recommend you move back to Calgary, near family and friends where you get the support and company of others." The doctor wrote a prescription for her, a mild sedative for night time.

They moved back to Calgary when Ed was to attend another six weeks at the technical institute, SAIT. After another short stay with Ed's folks they got the idea of care-taking an apartment block.

"Ed, I will have a job and still be able to care for Kari. We will pay less rent and have a nicer place to live—perfect, right honey?" Ed agreed. After his third year of his welding theory, he worked for a short time at his trade back in Calgary. He was building up hours needed to test for his B Pressure ticket.

Soon, after settling in, and working in the ten suites, building, the owner's behavior towards Chris put her on alert.

Mr. Schwartz, at least twice Chris' age, with a wife and a grown family, invited her to swim with him, at the Holiday Inn .

"Who else will be there?" Chris asked. *I hope he replies with 'My family and yours, too, of course, are invited.'* She had visions of her and Ed being treated as respected employees, introduced to his family and friends.

He answers, "Well ...other guests at the hotel of course."

A new vision crept into Chris' mind, shoving away the grandiose hope of hobnobbing in style. Inside her awakened familiar feelings—queasiness, loathing, and contempt for the bald, short, fat man. *How dare he try to tempt me into lewd behavior with him by dangling a lure––swimming at the Holiday Inn? Do I have to treat him nice in order to keep our care-taker position and our nice apartment? How do I handle this?*

"This week is bad timing. I am taking my daughter to a birthday party and I have promised to babysit for a friend the rest of the days but thank you for inviting me."

I need time to think of something better to say. A couple of weeks later he called to ask if this was a better time for swimming.

"Gee....Ed is working day shift this week. When he works night shift next week he can come too. Both of us will like it very much, thank you," she spilled out her rehearsed answer, "Just let us know when it's best for you, and we may have to bring our little girl too."

"Eh? Oh, ah…. I'm unable to go the following week."

What am I doing to invite this kind of attention? My Mum would say 'I told you so.' I won't mention this to her

When Chris' second pregnancy was evident Mr. Schwartz never invited again.

CHAPTER 47

Dean was born at 7:30 in the morning on May 27, 1968 at the Calgary Grace Maternity Hospital. At 8 o'clock in the morning of the same day, Erling was scheduled for amputation of his leg at the Calgary General Hospital. Ava visited Erling early afternoon then went to visit Chris after. She sat at Chris' bedside. Ava was morose and her visit depressed Chris. She felt robbed of the happy feeling of giving birth, influenced by Ava's mood. Chris felt helpless, not able to soothe her mother in any way. She didn't know how. They sat in oppressive silence.

When Ava took her leave, Chris wept for Erling. She wept for the family. She wept foreboding tears for bad times, yet to come.

For two weeks she had a perfect excuse—her own confinement after giving birth. With heavy dread in her heart, she agreed to accompany Ava on a hospital visit. After the bus ride, Ava headed off to the bathroom at the hospital. Chris approached Erling unnoticed. He sat in a wheel chair with his stump wrapped and resting on the support frame, staring out into nothingness. Desperate, Chris felt the need to be anywhere but here.

He turned his head around, smiled and in a weak voice, he said, "Hi Chris, good to see you, congratulations, a boy eh?"

"How are you? Are they treating you good?"

"Oh, I'm okay. Sure, the nurses are cute. Dey gives me vhiskey twice a day. Good for my circulation you know."

"You look thin. You have lost a lot of weight, I think."

"A leg veighs a lot, ja?" he laughed—a weak attempt at humor.

"Tomorrow I lose more weight. They didn't take enough, still infected. They have to cut quite a bit more."

Overcome with compassion Chris knew she was in trouble as her tears spilled over. She held his hand. He said nothing more. His tears spilled also. Chris never saw him cry before. Just then, Ava caught them in their shared moment.

"You two make a fine pair, Ja. Vat does tears help any of dis? It's a good ting I'm strong. Stop blubbering, you two. Stop feeling sorry and start figuring out how I vil get enough money to pay for everyting. I should be de one crying."

Erling told Ava to go home and not to come back to see him again. Chris brokenly said good-bye, unable to turn off her tears. People in the hospital lobby looked at her, so did the bus passengers.

Ava said, "You are embarrassing me with all dat crying. Stop now, everybody is looking." Ava never let up. She filled Chris in on the gruesome and hopeless situation of the family's finances.

Chris felt the need to take action, and fix things. The next day, she called Social Services. A worker visited with Chris and among tearful explanations she begged for

Social services to get help for the family. The worker called Ava and set up an appointment. At first Ava believed it was the hospital that contacted Welfare on the family's behalf. When she learned Chris was the instigator, she scolded, "Your dad vil be furious. He vil not take welfare, ja, you know him. You are in trouble now!"

"I don't care what you say or what he thinks. This is the only way I can help. We don't have enough money to give you. There is no shame in this help at this time." No more was said on the subject again. Help they got.

When Erling was close to discharge from hospital, he came home a day at a time—a trial run for the purpose of discovering how to manage.

On his first day, Ed drove him home. Chris stayed at her parent's house waiting nervously with the family and preparing the roast dinner Ed and her splurged for. The house, a bi-level presented quite an obstacle course for Erling to master entering—the stairs, his enemy. He got inside, weak and tired. After resting awhile, he decided to relax outside in the back yard, "I vaunt to practice the stairs."

"Chris, quick bring us towels, hurry up, Erling is hurt," Ed yelled.

Oh no! Oh God, What! Chris shifted into high gear and produced the towels.

"I forgot I had no leg, I forgot, I forgot," Erling's facial contortions revealed the agonizing pain he was in. Ed and Ava supported and wrapped the blood dripping stump. Instead of working the crutches as he should have done, Erling stepped out as if his leg was still there. He fell down with all his weight on the tender stump. Ed rushed him back to the hospital. The anticipated celebration turned somber and depressing.

The day came, Erling was home to stay, he walked across the yard and up the steps, sure footed, master of his prosthesis, sporting a proud grin. By his actions and comments it was clear to all he did not want pity. He proceeded to build a garage in the back yard and soon returned to his job.

CHAPTER 48

Chris was expected to spend Mothers' Day with Ava. The thought of it gnawed at her, into her inner depths—her mind, body, and soul. *A phony, that's me, a real phony.* She bought the card and went to the house. She styled Ava's hair and cooked dinner. All the while, she watched the clock, counting the time left until her escape, when Ed would pick her up.

"De lawn is looking brown and needs somting but I don't know vat to do. I can't do everyting around here," Ava whined. Chris knew this was an opener for her to take up the challenge.

"Ed just fertilized the lawn at the apartment and it looks real good after lots of watering. Maybe your lawn needs it too."

"Dere is no money for fertilizer around here, not enough money for anyting."

"We had a little left over. Maybe we can give it to you," Chris offered, feeling she saved the day and came through with something to appease her mother.

"Do you tink Ed will put it on for me?"

"I will ask him."

"Ask him, he should offer. You guys don't vaunt to do anything for me. FORGET IT!"

"Mother, for God's sake, what's the matter with you? Ed is not mine to command to do what I want or what you want. If I don't ask him, how is he to know?"

"He can see de grass is brown. FORGET IT!" Her face went beet-red. Her eyes were mere slits. Huffing, she stomped over to the phone desk, grabbed the card Chris had given her and ripped it to shreds and threw it in Chris' face, and the pieces fluttered down, and landed at her feet. Calm, with tears streaming down her face, Chris infuriated Ava, as her tears always did. Chris picked up the ruined card, a rejection by her mother one more time. She took it to the garbage can as if to show her mother what she thought of their relationship. She went directly to the phone, "Ed, please pick me up right away!"

*****

Ed returned to Fort McMurray for a time. Chris pleaded for change. Ed recognized he too was missing out on his young family. They agreed they did not want to spend time apart. They embarked on a voyage of many moves following Oil Patch work around the oil rich province of Alberta.

CHAPTER 49

Jubilant and with goose bumps, Chris greeted Ed at the door, anxious, and in need of sharing the good news. She wished for him to be as happy as she was about her Bedstemor and Bedstefar coming to Canada for a visit.

"Ed, my Grandparents are coming to Canada and bringing Moster—my Bedstemor's sister. You will love them. You will have proof I have nice relatives too."

Ed listened and smiled, "great hon."

"But Ed, there's a real problem here. I want to spend all the time with them when they are here and how can I now we're on this job far from Calgary? I can't invite them to this motel."

"We'll go visit."

"Visit? It's not good enough! I need more time with them. If only your mum and dad were in their own house instead of it being rented out—I could stay with them and be close. Oh what will I do?" Happy, yet sad, Chris lay in bed trying to find a solution.

"Ed, wake up, I have an idea, I know how."

"Chris, for God's sake, what is it?"

"I'll ask if I can stay right there with them in my parent's house. You know they have a box spring and mattress of that corner in the basement. I can sleep there and there is room for you when you come to visit. We can put Dean's crib there and there's my old bed there, too, for Kari. It can work. There's lots of room."

"Are you out of your mind? You can't stay there and feel good about it, remember?"

"Ava will behave when others are around. Besides I will put up with anything to be with my Grandparents. Please, Ed. Agree with me on this, it means a lot to me?"

Everyone agreed. Chris was ecstatic. They moved in before the arrival and she went to the airport. What fun they had. Bedstemor and her sister were cheerful and goofy most of the time. Bedstefar gave the atmosphere serenity and calmness. They approved of Ed right away when they met him, even though they didn't share a language. They communicated with hand signals and much playacting, giggling and nodding to each other. Chris toured them by bus, around Calgary, while the two older women shopped for souvenirs. A routine developed on the stay at home days. Ava took an afternoon nap almost every day as Bedstefar did too. The three others sunned in the back yard, relaxing and talking in Danish about everything while watching Wendy, Kari, and Dean playing. It was hot weather at the time and Bedstemor who only wore dresses stripped down to her slip. On one such afternoon, Bedstemor brought up the subject about Chris' real father, astounding her. No one ever wanted to talk about it before.

"Kirsten, has your mother told you anything about your dad in Denmark?—You do know, don't you?"

"Oh! I am happy you will talk about it because I am not allowed to, with them."

Chris related the incident about the letter announcing Mrs. Kjaer's death and the scene between her mother and herself. She let it all out, "I have always felt different, shameful because it is a secret. Bedste tell me too about my Mother and what she was like growing up. I don't understand her ways."

Chris learned Ava was different in behavior from her sisters. She had acted bossy and mean towards them. Ava's younger sister had been afraid of her, like the time Ava locked her in a closet for a long time. Bedstemor herself, had trouble understanding Ava's moods.

"All I want is to know what there is to know, and I dream about meeting him. I have always felt no one would ever understand my pain or my need."

"Kirsten, I am telling you there was a trust fund for you in Denmark, a bank account, for you to have later on. Bedstefar had the right to administer it on your behalf. When Ava and Erling decided to move to Canada they told Bedstefar they wanted the money as a loan to pay for the trip over. They guaranteed to pay you back one day and I am telling you this because Bedstefar feels bad you might not get it. Your real dad signed paternity papers, guaranteeing child support plus inheritance rights. Mark my words, my girl, and pay attention to what I am saying. One day you will have money coming and you must make sure you get it. I know you have not always been treated right. You have known sadness and loneliness. One day you will be rewarded but you must go after it for if you don't, others will just laugh at your stupidity."

"But....I don't want anything. I don't want to be selfish or mean. I guess I just want to know him, be one of his family members. That's what I want."

"Sounds nice but it won't be that way. I hope you change your mind. You deserve something. You deserve lots!"

Six weeks passed way too fast for Chris. The day came for good-byes. Chris' tears did not stop, not even when Ava sent dirty looks in her direction. She felt enormous loss, depression and surety that she saw her grandparents for the last time.

*****

Chris rejoined Ed on the road and the next visit to Calgary was at Christmas. Christmas Eve was with her folks, and Christmas Day with his. While at her parents' house she noticed how much, Erling and Ava came to enjoy good-night kisses from her little ones—a ritual that Kari and Dean were used to at bed time from everyone around them.

Work west of Edmonton for Ed offered them the opportunity to strike further out and away—new town, new friends, and new experiences. This brought Chris to think more about her future, and not to dwell on her past. One particular day she held a private ceremony dealing with her personal demons, one she came to regret many times because it did not wipe out the depression she felt about her childhood. Bedstemor had brought Dolly Lise and the lamb for her, after keeping them in Denmark until the time she might get there herself to pick them up. The doll and the lamb were now yellowed with age, Chris wondered if they might harbor disease or bugs, never mind the painful memories they invoked in her. *I will hold a funeral for these things and my sad thoughts.* She tossed them in the burning barrel and watched them go up in flames.

CHAPTER 50

Ava and Erling moved out of Alberta, to Vancouver Island, bought a car wash and later a Laundromat. This was an attempt at a job for both, easier for Erling, a milder climate with less snow for him to deal with. These businesses proved unsuccessful. Ava went back to working with the mentally challenged in an institution. Erling found employment as a repair man for small motors and appliances.

Once a year, Chris and Ed travelled to British Columbia or Erling and Ava drove to Alberta. Their visits always involved alcohol. Ava and Erling never stopped before all of it was consumed or they passed out. They had heated arguments with one another. Ava belittled Erling and yelled insults at him for their plight, "I am sick and tired of taking care of everyone all de time. At vork I have to take care of people and at home, ja, all my life. Vel, I am sick of it, do you hear me? Sick of it! Does anybody care about me? No! Nobody cares! I can't vait until I get to go to a nursing home one day and have dem take care of me! I hate dat wheel chair and those damn crutches of yours. Maybe I can go to the moon and be by myself."

"Mum, don't say such things. You can't mean it.

"Vat do you know, just wait and see your time is coming."

Hurtful conversations were all they had. Whenever Chris attempted any subject, mum turned negative and Chris was more apprehensive and nervous at the mere thought of spending time with her. Always she hoped the visits one way or the other was avoidable but guilt and obligation won every time. However, her nervousness became unbearable and just a week prior to their next arrival she went to her doctor and asked for a prescription to help her relax, "I need to sleep. I need to stop quaking inside and stop my tongue from shivering."

"Why do you suppose you react this way?"

"It's my Mum. It has never been right between us but now it is worse."

The doctor fished for something else, "I have experience with hypnosis and if you are willing I suggest you consider this therapy. It may well help you in dealing with your nervousness and at least understand it better. It may not be your mother at all. Anything is better than relying on drugs for masking a problem."

"Okay if you recommend it. I am willing. If only I can fix this."

On leaving his office Chris came away with guilt feelings, *somehow it's my fault, not Mum's.*

The evening came for the hypnosis session and the fact it was outside regular clinic hours lent an eerie sneaky feeling to the already unfamiliar tension of what lay ahead.

Despite the doctor telling Chris she would not recall what happened under hypnosis, she did.

She could not move. She lay as if paralyzed. The doctor asked her several easy to answer questions and she did with calmness. At mention of the word father she became hysterical, shivered and shook.

The doctor stopped and brought her out of the trance and when she calmed down, the doctor said, "My dear, your behavior under hypnosis leads me to believe you must have been abused by your step dad when you were young. Most probably you have no conscious memory of this because it causes too much trauma for you."

"No way—Nothing at all like it happened," Chris said. "You have misunderstood. I remember you telling me not to remember while under hypnosis. Why do I remember everything you said?"

"I am not sure why, but I don't think we shall continue this time. Perhaps we will clear things more the next time," the doctor said.

"Well, I'll think about it and let you know if I want to come again." She knew that she did not want any more of his therapy and was quick to be on her way out of there.

*****

Some friends reacted with shock if Chris revealed her feelings towards her mother. One friend, Joyce, said, "How can you say you hate your mother? She can't be that bad. My mother is a terrific person I can't imagine a mother who is not." Chris felt ashamed and gave it great thought and agreed it sounded awful. She decided to paint a picture, with words. Her spoken words from then on became more of a generic excuse—An excuse covering all circumstances.

"My Mum and I have not gotten along well at all, for most of my life, for one reason or another." Then she dismissed the subject.

Erling and Ava came for one of their visits causing Chris great anguish, wishing she didn't have to see Ava again. Ava was sneaking their liquor then watering it down. Ava insisted Chris stay up with her awhile, to talk she said. Out of obligation and curiosity Chris obeyed the order. Ava produced paternity papers, signed by Chris' father.

"I guess it's time you take care of dese yourself now. Ja, and act on your inheritance ven de time comes and make sure you do. If you don't you are very stupid. Ja, he deserves to pay," she shook her finger with anger, and a cruel look to her drunken face. Chris felt her mother would depend on her to take up the fight of revenge against her father.

"Mother, please tell me about you and my real dad. I need to know."

"Vee lived together for a couple of years. He was a spoiled brat, selfish, mean, he drank a lot."

Chris didn't believe her. The story didn't fit her fantasy. She didn't say much, only encouraged her mother to go on.

"I got pregnant by him again ven you vere two years old. Vee was going to get married but I knew it as a

190

mistake. Ja, I had an abortion and called it quits. Later, he came crawling, begging me to take him back. His parents vere kind to you and his modder always asked to see you. Sombody in deir family, vitout children vanted to adopt you but I didn't him to be near you at all. You are lucky I kept you.

The venom in her voice agitated Chris. She wanted to escape to bed and hear no more. But, Ava was on a roll. She had her daughter's attention.

"I haven't had an easy life and you don't know all of it eider. Vel, I vil tell you somting ellers."

Chris didn't want to listen anymore. She didn't want to feel responsible for her mother's misery anymore, "Please let's go to bed. It's late," Chris stood up.

"No, vait one minute, Ja," it seemed Ava forgot what she was going to say. She hesitated not sure…then "Ven young I vork in hotel, war started. De Nazis came, ja, and took over hotel—make us do vat dey ," her speech slurred, it was difficult to understand. Her eyes were closing.

Chris dismissed further conversation. It was bed time. Ava never spoke to Chris again regarding her father or the Nazis and the hotel. It was again not to talk about. Lying in bed, thinking back on their conversation her thoughts went in many directions. *If, she knew I already contacted my real dad—I can't begin thinking how the conversation might have turned out. She will never know if I can help it.*

CHAPTER 51

Her cousin, Nita, lived in the same town as Chris' father. She sent an advertisement for his business, after Chris asked her to find a connection.

Chris' first letter to her father was difficult to write, even to mail. She introduced her immediate family, included pictures, and took care not to mention Ava. She explained how she felt the need to know herself better by making contact with her biological father. Time passed. Anxious, but eager she checked her mail, every day. When his letter arrived, she stared at it for a long time, turned it over, studied front and back. She savored the wait before opening the letter. She read it, read it again. *A letter for me from my father—imagine his touch, here,*

Her letter surprised him. He had thought of her at times over the years. He believed Chris would not have heard anything good about him. He admitted at the time he was too young and irresponsible. His wife, Ruth, knew about his daughter with Ava but, their three children did not—he wanted them to be older before informing them.

Chris was disappointed he requested she must write to him at his business address and not show her return address on the outside of the envelope. The explanation was Ruth's jealousy, even though Chris was born before he met her. He did not want her upset. He sent a picture of himself, signed it C.C., which his friends called him. He requested she refer to him the same way.

A secret, a big fat secret—me, a not to talk about, me—Chris' heart ached more than ever before. *I will never correspond with him again, except for one last word.*

Dear CC

Thank you for the picture you sent, which I have studied with great interest. It was exciting to hear from you but not without disappointment for me. I do not want to cause discord for you or your family. Your request of writing in secret is a sure way to promote misery for all, if it becomes known. I have always resented the secrecy around my paternity. For you to ask me to remain a secret—a hush-hush subject—I have decided not to write again.

Kirsten

Wow! Chris' heart raced—within a month another letter came. No other envelope, hand-writing, or stamp looked as dear to her as this one. *He actually wrote to me again.* Weeping, she sat with his letter in her hands for a long time. Tears of relief and joy eased from the innermost depth of her soul. He apologized. He had told Ruth about Chris' letter. Chris was invited to write whenever she wished.

The ten years, from 1976 to 1986, they corresponded together a couple of times a year. He always signed C.C. Chris signed Kirsten.

CHAPTER 52

At her home, in Victoria, Ava hid full and empty liquor bottles. She drank her black coffee with vodka in it. Everyone knew it but, it's not to talk about.

Chris had anxiety problems again on a Christmas Eve afternoon at her parent's home. Her heart was not in coming but the obligatory monster took its hold and here they were.

Erling and Ed, with Erling's buddies, stopped in for cheer at the local pub after a bit of Christmas shopping. The kids, Ava, and Chris were at home while the traditional Danish meal was cooking. Ava, irritated, cursed and condemned the men who are late. Chris did her best to smooth it over, "They won't be real late. They know it's Christmas. Please don't be angry—it's upsetting the kids."

"Here I am, always slaving avay and nobody gives a damn about me, just take me for granted all de time," Ava kept on sneaking spirits into her coffee cup.

Intoxicated and wild by the time the guys returned, Ava flung herself at them when they came through the door and hurled verbal insults.

"Stop it Ava, stop it right now, for the kids" said Erling

Ava sulking gave the silent treatment all through dinner. During gift opening she refused to open her presents. "I don't vant anything from any of you."

Her statement brought on such fury, a brawling melee ensued. Karl punched a big hole in a wall.

194

It seemed as though all got sucked into a whirlwind of bad behavior. Adults were all yelling, pushing, shoving, threatening—too insane to describe it all.

Chris and Ed packed up and left. They took their children out of there and vowed never to speak to Ava again.

Chris took a difficult but brave action.

"I am finished with mother I don't understand how you keep living with her. I have to tell you—I often thought you should divorce her. Don't bring her to visit at my house again." Chris said to Erling over the phone after they arrived back home.

During the time of banishment, Erling came out alone once, to celebrate his birthday with Chris and family. Ava went to Denmark. Chris wondered how she behaved with her sisters.

One and a half years passed then Erling called to ask if Ava was welcome. He promised good behavior on her part.

CHAPTER 53

Often, a melancholy mood overtook Chris. She wept for the past. She wept for the present. She wept with worry for the future. She lost sleep and was often depressed. She found it difficult to snap out of it. Chris put a lot of energy, love and care into nurturing relationships with her siblings. *Together as adults we will share happy times. We will build strong bonds and blissful memories. I am lucky Ed supports my decisions and opens his heart and home to help my younger siblings whenever I want to.*

*****

Karl had dropped out of school and planned to head for Bella Coola to find work. Chris intervened, and asked Ed to help find him work in a trade in Alberta and at least get a trade certificate. He roomed and boarded with them off and on

Karl started as an Ironworker apprentice. He paid his way to cover his board. The mobile home the family lived in was cramped. They made a move to Spruce Grove, bought a house and Karl got a room in the basement. Chris went to Beauty School to complete her Beautician Certificate. Kari and Dean were unhappy there and missed their old school and friends. The family decided to sell, and move back and Chris could open a hair salon there. Karl was given notice it was time—he should become independent. They spent just one Christmas in the big house. Kris' memories of her childhood—the farm, and all the relatives in Denmark, forever on her mind, led the way for planning the event. She wanted the food the same, served according to tradition. She included traditions from Erling's side as well—lots of shopping, cooking, and baking. Every little detail was taken care of, with love.

Behind Chris' façade her nerves played havoc. She saw a doctor and took the usual sedative for the duration of the upcoming visit. This time Ava did behave, and Ed and

Chris hosted a huge traditional four day event, with many guests.

Karl and Laura met and married a few months after he was told it was time he moved out. Karl, intoxicated, walked down the aisle at their wedding. He fought with his best man the night before. Time passed, Laura sported a black eye. She revealed the truth, after she first lied about walking into a door. Karl hit her in a fit of anger. He became known as a bully. Once, he jumped on the running board of a truck, punched the driver in the face during a union strike. Television news cameras captured the event. Chris' feelings for Karl changed. She used to feel protective towards him. Now she feared him. She still loved, and needed him, but in the way she used to fantasize about family relationships...

CHAPTER 54

How strange it is, I am now an example Ava expects the other children to follow. Chris heard resentment from the younger ones. She understood that as normal. But, her Mother, using her for the role model for her younger children she didn't understand.

"Chris cleaned the house," or "Chris cooked," or "Chris did well in School," etcetera—the younger ones repeated, with sarcasm and mockery.

Communication by letters, continued to flow between C.C. and Chris, they shared much about themselves.

C.C.'s initials stood for Carl Christian. Kirsten went by Chris because often she was Christine or Christen. *Strange, I chose spelling Chris, with a C instead of a K. It's as if I was always tied to him in some sort of way.* She opened a hair salon business and named it 'Chris' Hair Care.'

When they moved to Red Deer where she worked as a stylist in a senior's apartment and received checks made payable to Chris. The bank approached her. Her account was in the name of Kirsten, a discrepancy. In all legal documents she used Kirsten. From that day on she felt she reclaimed a small part of her own identity. She began spelling Kris with a K. If she was referred to as Kirsten and pronounced it Kiersten she was happy. If they pronounced it Kursten she wanted to correct them, sometimes she did.

CHAPTER 55

Erling suffered a heart attack. He was in intensive care in the Victoria Hospital. "The ambulance came because I called for dem. Ja, tank me, he is alive. He was dead, I saved him. I might not have done dat," Ava agitated, reached for a refill of whiskey, "you guys care more about him den about me!"

The group of four entered the house moments before her tirade began. The drive from Alberta to British Columbia was almost non-stop except for fuel and toilet time. Kris' brother, Karl and his wife Laura shared the drive with her and Ed after Ava called. They felt it best to get there as quickly as possible, and drove straight to the hospital in Victoria.

Erling, in intensive care, showed obvious happiness at seeing all of them. The fact they came, he said, was all he needed to get better and return home. Against the advice of his doctor, he did check himself out within a couple of days and resumed his smoking and drinking.

Kris had questions for him, "Do you remember anything? Did you see a white light?"

"No, I was pretty drunk and dat might explain vhy I have no memory."

"Gee, I have always felt afraid of death. I am always searching for evidence to comfort me."

"Vel I won't live as long as you dat's for sure. I vil send you a message if I can when I get dere." They laughed about it but Kris felt serious about it, at the same time.

Erling wanted his ashes scattered in a favorite spot of his in British Columbia.

Kris loved watching birds. To her they represented peace. "I want my ashes placed in the base of a heavy ornamental bird bath, sitting in an idyllic place with hummingbird feeders nearby," Kris told Erling

The whole time the four of them spent out there, Ava was at her worst. She made it obvious she was jealous of the attention Erling received. Her behavior created tension beyond belief. She was a walking time bomb and she did explode the night before Erling came home. She always refused to accompany us to visit him, "he has you and he don't need me, I'll have him back soon enough making more vork for me," Ava grumbled.

While they visited Erling, she sat home, drinking, and fuming with negative, vindictive thoughts. They were just in the door and she started needling Karl about Wendy's bad behavior, "I tink Vendy stole my gold nugget necklace. Who can do somting about her? I don't know hov to handle her."

When Karl was fueled with alcohol he stormed Wendy physically, accused her, and demanded an explanation. This scene took place in the back garden. Ed and Kris went out to try to calm the yelling. Ava was upstairs in her bedroom peeking out. Kris saw a look of pure evil delight, a cold expression making her shiver. *This is my family—Thank God my children did not come with us this time.* Ed, Laura and Kris tried to calm things but, without success.

Ava soon appeared, stomping, yelling insults and accusations at Wendy, riling the situation to a feverish pitch. Kris stepped in front of her and blocked the punch intended for Wendy. Kris, her feet firmly planted, squeezed Ava's wrist, and she held her Mother's fiery gaze, "Stop it, right now! Stop it!" Kris demanded.

"I HATE YOU. JA, I HATE YOU!" Ava, hissed through clenched teeth with eyes narrowed, piercing, boring through Kris as if she might knock her down. Kris' strength ebbed away. Ava said it. She said what Kris knew all along. She walked away, Ed followed. They left the others to handle the situation.

CHAPTER 56

When the subject of Christmas, came up, Kris felt helpless. Erling and Ava wanted to come once again. It was 1983 and Kris planned and worked towards setting the scene for an idyllic holiday. Ed and Kris lived in a brand new home, settled in Red Deer. It would be their first Christmas there. While having coffee, with a neighbor, Debbie, Kris confessed how nervous she was about having her relatives come for Christmas. *I must not get into any of it. I recall looks of disapproval on people's faces in the past.* Debbie reassured her with talk of how normal nervousness is, "I get nervous too, then it all works out, just fine.

Just awful, was how. They finished the Christmas Eve meal. Kris dressed up as Mrs. Claus planning to pass out the gifts. Good friends, Bob and Marge stopped in for a visit along with their daughter, Carol and her husband, Barry. They enjoyed drinks and chatter all around. Carol and Barry left, leaving behind a group of fourteen.

Surprised and worried, Chris saw Wendy rush, to the basement and Karl stormed after her. Their yelling and cursing began. Confused, Kris did not know what this was about. Back up they came. Karl grabbed Wendy by the hair. Erling bellowed Karl's name.

201

Ed put a hand on Karl's shoulder, "Not in my house, Karl, STOP, right now," Ed said in firm voice. Karl made an abrupt turn, began pummeling Ed with his huge fists.

Instinctively, Kris threw her arms around Karl's neck, "Please Karl, control yourself!" "Please look at me Karl, please. Her stomach was tied in knots. She feared the worst, but, tried making eye contact with him. He let go of Ed, managed to push Kris into a corner.

His eyes wild, drilled into hers, his teeth gritted, lips quivered—he appeared as a maniacal monster, and he hissed, "You think you are damned perfect, you and your perfect family, perfect house, perfect friends. You guys make me sick. Why do you bother to invite me anyway?"

Kris and Ed's son, Dean, jumped on Karl's back, wanting to protect his mother. Ed and Karl started brawling. Blood smeared the walls. Kris went for the phone, called the police.

Laura ran for their belongings, ordered her two girls into the car and managed to convince Karl he must get out of there before the cops arrived. Gone just in time, Kris' brother left behind a house full of scars, three huge holes in the walls, scratched paint and bloody walls.

"Do you want to press charges?" The police asked after the situation was explained to them.

"No, what good will come of it? No! He's my family, I can't," Kris protested.

*****

Deep, and dark, depression wrapped around Kris. She began mending her home. Layers of putty, hours of drying, sanding, painting, she wept often through it all as her thoughts remembered how she used to fantasize happy relationships with her grown up siblings. *I manage to set the stage, provide all the props. I write the script in my head and it dances around. I hope and pray all will go right. I must stop. When will I stop allowing the evil into my family, by allowing them into our lives?* Kris couldn't recall what Ava did during the fight. She imagined she stood by, smug, enjoying the scene.

CHAPTER 57
DENMARK

In just a few short hours I will stand on the ground of my beloved birth country. Kris felt great pride for anything Danish. *Now twenty six years later after I left here I am at last getting to come back.* She reached for the crook of Ed's arm and gave it a squeeze, "l look forward to taking you around this country so you may experience Denmark through your own senses instead of listening to me go on and on. Just a few more hours, I'm getting excited." Ed smiled back at her put his hand over hers and gave it a big warm squeeze.

All the relatives, including Erling's side, lavished welcoming gestures on them. They soaked it all up with much appreciation. Erling's brother loaned them a car and they toured all over in it including a trip to Germany, as far as West Berlin. They saw more of Denmark than a lot of Danes ever saw in their life time.

*****

Dearest to Kris' heart, were the people and places in and around Ribe—She could have kissed the cobblestone ground she walked on. It was a ground with layers and layers of refuse and rubbish underneath the cobblestone. Ribe, a medieval town was the earliest trading center in seven hundred AD. Coziness exuded everywhere. Kris wanted to re-explore every alley, nook and cranny as she and Ed meandered through Kris' childhood memories. Without a wrong turn, Kris was an able guide. Nothing had changed except there were different people in the houses. Enveloped in feelings of comfort and love, Kris took it all in and confirmed her memories. It was as though her Bedstemor walked beside her. They drove out in the country to Lustrup, stopped at the same little confectionery and Kris recognized the owner behind the counter. An older man now but he was still recognizable. Kris introduced her-self to him. He remembered and spoke with fondness about her grandparents. She was awestruck how something can be the same as it appeared when they pulled into the farm yard. The white washed, three sided building, with a thatched roof looked no different. There was one big, important exception.

"Do you want to go inside?" someone asked.

"I don't think…no…No…Bedste will not be there, sitting at her end of the table, coffee cup in hand…No…If only, they both still lived."

*****

As Kris, critical and meticulous, turned in front of the mirror, her psyche seemed in a different place, detached. Ed had left on a sightseeing tour with Uncle Soren. Kris made excuses— she needed solitude, time to pull herself together or as her Mother often said, 'time to find myself.' Kris' hand shook and the mascara smeared. Too much anyway, she decided and wiped her face clean then started again. *I can't appear without make-up. Besides brightening up my face it gives me confidence.*

When she felt satisfied she joined her Aunt Inger downstairs, and she greeted Kris with warmth and understanding for the bad case of jittery nerves that Kris confessed to suffer from.

This is a momentous day in my life—the day I meet my real father. He is expecting me at four o'clock as arranged by the phone call I placed to him a few days ago," Kris told Aunt Inger.

With her heart thumping, her knees weak, and her mind shouting, *No Tears*! She prepared to etch the scene, everlasting, into her memory.

Kris' eyes photographed CC's face, searched for recognition of herself, his face her mirror. They connected, eyes locked and they shared a hand shake.

"You look like your mother," was CC's first comment.

Just leave her out of this. I do not want her with me today, out loud she said, "Oh," followed by a nervous short giggle.

Formal, friendly, and in typical Danish tradition CC guided them into his home, to the coffee table waiting, set for tea.

"I am a tea drinker but I will gladly make you coffee if you prefer?" CC spoke in English and continued, "Please excuse my wife for not greeting you today. This is still difficult for Ruth."

Sadness crept into Kris' heart and mind. *If only Ruth would agree to meet me, surely she would then realize I'm not meaning to be a disruptive threat to Ruth, CC, or their children.*

They chatted back and forth about the flight over, and what she had experienced to date. She showed photos of her home and family. CC produced a few albums with pictures of his wife and children setting names to the pictures. Included were photographs of his parents and grandparents. These photos aroused Kris' curiosity. *These folks are my own bloodline revealed after all these years.*

CC offered a tour of his large rambling home. Kris was impressed by his art collection lining the long hallway designed to be his own private art gallery. She learned he enjoyed painting and showed her five works he had painted. There was a garden scene, a small stream, with an old brick bridge crossing over the water. Two paintings were bright color abstracts but the one CC commented on was a nude painting of his wife, painted as she looked in her youth. Kris fought to hide her surprised amazement. 'Wow' she thought to herself, t*his father of mine is formal, well mannered, and educated but not as old fashioned as I imagined him to be. He was obviously open-minded. Kris*

206

mused awhile about Ruth. Did she ever object to people looking at this painting?

A stroll on his property revealed the pride and love CC cultivated in his impressive surroundings. Kris liked him, admired him. Her fantasies were confirmed, and she felt rejuvenated, proud of her father. CC, explained, Kris listened and she complemented the flora as they walked on paths that lead through a manicured vegetable garden, and an ornate fragrant rose garden, bordered by a variety of shrubs and trees. When they reached an idyllic shady retreat flanked by statues and a lily pond, CC motioned to Kris they should sit down,

"This is my favorite place to relax, read a book or meditate," he reached out and patted Kris' hand, "I will speak with Ruth about arranging another visit here with our children present. I think you will like to meet them and I believe they will want to meet you too. I will phone you."

He asked Kris many questions about her life, happiness, career, and her family. Kris' mental state soared with deep gratitude. Her heart pumped with love for this man who was just as she imagined throughout her childhood. CC's facial expression spoke of genuine interest in her, a parental concern she seldom felt in her life except perhaps when she was in the care of her dear Bedstemor, in the past.

An awkward silence fell over the two of them when questions and answers seemed to come to an end. CC once again reached out and took Kris' hand and held it between his own.

"I have suffered guilt for having a child I never took a chance to be a father to. I don't know what your mother has told you about me but it probably is nothing good. I was young, reckless, a real girl chaser, not wanting to settle down. Your mother and I came together a couple of times for agreeable, consensual sex after meeting at a dance. You may feel disappointed it was almost a one night stand and not a romantic affair. I barely knew your mother."

"I am happy you are truthful with me, I appreciate it," Kris replied.

"Please tell me about your growing up years, in Denmark and in Canada too? Tell me about your step Father. Tell me all you will share with me so I may know you better."

Indeed, an invitation came. For Kris it was a momentous occasion. She couldn't begin to imagine what it meant to the others. She assumed their feelings varied. CC, Ruth, their three children, and Kris posed for a snap shot, Ed was the photographer.

I must be grateful for this time and this photo for this may be all there ever will be.

*****

They carried on touring, saw things, unimaginable, in Hamburg and Berlin. They drove into these cities, checked into a hotel, and booked a day and a night tour through the reception desk. Their naiveté was by many degrees lessened. Unbelievable, was the entertainment, in red light districts. They discussed how they lived in a puritan country. Standing near the Berlin wall was frightening, as was travel, in and out of East Germany. Upon their return to Denmark, Ed commented how good it felt to be at home again, in a place, where at least one of them was capable of speaking and reading the language.

They travelled Denmark from East to West—from the southernmost part of Jutland to the northern tip at Skagen where two oceans meet. Many tourists took their pictures there and Kris posed for a snap shot with Erling's brother, Helge.

A lifelong dream came true and the trip exceeded all expectations.

CHAPTER 58
CANADA

Jet-lagged and drugged from a sleeping pill, Kris reached for the irritating phone. Almost midnight, the clock reveals. She is not happy with the wake-up call. *How many people actually know we are home?*

Kris heard his drunken words difficult to understand, "Hallo, you got home, ha, how vas it?" Erling asked, "Did you meet him?" Kris stiffened, her mind stuck on his last question. She was unprepared and overwhelmed, *whatever happened to the not to talk about attitude? Lie, play dumb, deny, tell him whatever he wants to hear but oh God, please help me?* Kris' brain kicked into gear. She spoke, slow, deliberate, pushing the guilt away. "Yes, I met him and everything was fine. You woke us up, we are really worn out. Thank you for calling, I will call you back tomorrow night."

For their next conversation, Erling was sober and again it was back as 'not to talk about.'

The following Fathers' Day Kris wired her step father, flowers. They understood each other. He was ecstatic, "Tank you, I never had flovers before, nobody ever gave me flovers before, tank you." Kris wondered what went through her mother's mind.

Life moved on with minimal visits between Kris and her parents. Ed and Kris were in a state of personal problems, caused by business changes. They dealt with triumphs and tribulations of their near, adult children, and had their own 'tug of war' in keeping their marriage intact.

Their daughter, Kari, enrolled at the University of Victoria. She turned down the offer to stay with her grandparents. Kris decided to accompany her daughter on the drive out and fly home. Kari's room and board place did not have a bed for her—she decided to stay with her parents. Erling invited Kari and Kris for Saturday brunch, Danish style, meaning open faced sandwiches, beer and Akvavit.

"Vere the hell is my Akvavit?" Erling shouted from the entry where the freezer stood. Ava, was slicing tomatoes, hands shaking—she did not answer.

"Ava, Vendy!" Erling yelled again, "GOD, DAMN IT!" he cursed. Ava looked as if she might collapse. Kris approached her and took the knife out of her hand and proceeded with the tomatoes.

Erling and Wendy outside in the back yard yelled at each other. Wendy slammed through the back door, and raced up the stairs. Kris was dumbfounded, she didn't know what to say or what problem had just surfaced. Ava retreated up the stairs as well. Kris went outside and joined Erling. He inhaled deeply from his cigarette.

"What's wrong here?" Kris asked in a quiet tone of voice, "I don't understand what happened."

"My bottle of Akvavit, gone," he looked at her, while he wrung his large hands," dey're trying to tell me dat I drank it a long time ago. I am tired of living with those two, FUCKING ALCOHOLICS!"

"Never mind the Akvavit, we don't need it. Kari and I don't care. It's best we don't have any." They got through a strained brunch. The next day, Erling drove Kris to the airport. Before boarding her plane, he insisted on buying her a gift to take home, a box of British Columbia smoked salmon.

CHAPTER 59

February 18, 1990 Ava turned sixty-five. "I don't think we can make it. Ed can't take the time off," Kris explained to Erling.

"You have to come. Dat's all dere is to it. Do you hear me?" Erling replied in his strictest voice. Kris giggled a little and attempted once more to protest. He interrupted gruffly, "Your modder only turns sixty-five once. You get here for sure."

Obligation won again. Wendy who still lived at home attended but Karl did not. They did want to visit with Kari and that cured their trepidation.

The day they arrived, Ava flung the door open, eyes bleary. Her cheeriness gave away her drunken state.

"You finally did it, Ja," Ava slung the insult for taking a longtime for Kris to lose weight. She was used to her mother's remarks, regarding her appearance and didn't respond.

"Do somting with your hair. I don't like it. Ja, dat doesn't look good on you." Kris sat down in an easy chair and saw an empty beer bottle tucked under the drapery. If anything had changed, it was Ava's drinking was more severe.

Erling arrived home from work in a cab. His car was parked in the driveway. Strange, Kris thought. She cooked supper, Ava was too drunk. The nice thing about it was she disappeared early, and passed out. Erling got drunk but stayed pleasant. As Kris rose to go up to bed and walked near his chair, he reached out for her, "Please come here, sit down," he pulled Kris onto his lap, wrapped his arms tight around her and for a moment he hugged her tight, "Of all de kids, you are my favorite," his voice broke up, he struggled for composure.

Kris managed to say, "Oh sure, you tell that to all your kids, well...good night, I love you, too," she hurried up the stairs, touched by words she waited so long to hear, even though they weren't sober words.

Ava thought they were going out for a meal at her favorite high priced restaurant.

Kris wished it were that way—perhaps a better setting for acceptable behavior. Instead, a surprise, the party was planned for next door at a neighbor's. Kris sat near to Aunt Elma and Kari. She observed rapid drunkenness by the majority of persons there. Kris put in her time waiting for an acceptable time to retreat. When first she entered the neighbor's house Kris removed her shoes. Ava did not. As they passed, Kris' foot felt the high heel of Ava's shoe tearing through her stocking, piercing the skin, and bruising the flesh. Kris gasped in pain. Blood trickled between her toes.

Ava laughed, "Your feet are too big, get out of my vay."

Kris' foot burned but the stinging hateful remark hurt much worse. *If only I was not here!*

Wendy knelt ceremoniously in front of Ava's chair. "Dear Mom, I love you very much.. I will read my card out loud for everyone to hear," Wendy began, hesitated, and tapped Ava's knees, and continued through her mother's ill-mannered indifference. Wendy struggled, raised her voice, and reached the end, of the mushy purchased words. Deflated, she backed off. Kris was sorry for Wendy, and felt her embarrassment.

Elma, Kari, and Kris left early. The others stayed, and partied on.

Unable to sleep, agitated, foot hurting, and feeling home sick, Kris overheard Ava and Erling hurling words of accusation and denial regarding a certain bottle of whiskey. Kris gave in, got up, and fetched the whiskey she earlier on put out of sight, out of mind, she thought, "Here you are, get after it," Kris plunked the bottle on the table and retreated to bed, thinking of another time, another place.

CHAPTER 60

The next day, Ed and Kris visited the city of Nanaimo, and stayed at Ben and Elma's where Kris slept twelve blissful hours.

They continued on their planned extended vacation, and travelled down to Seattle, by ferry, out of Victoria and back there again for one more night's visit with Erling, Ava and Wendy. Erling wanted them to meet him downtown the next day for lunch, near his work.

Ed and Kris ordered a salad, but Erling only wanted coffee. Conversation did not come easy. Erling cleared his throat as if he had something important to say, his fingers drummed on the table top. Finally after a deep breath, he begun, "Ed, I vant to give you my table saw. I forgot to say it before. Vil you go back and put it in the back of your truck before you head for home?"

Ed blurted out, "You might still need it, Erling, thank you much though, maybe next time, if you still don't need it."

"I vont need it. I vant you to have it!"

"Thank you, next time." We took our leave, uncomfortable, unhappy somehow.

One month later, Erling was dead. He died in his sleep, THANK GOD!—He suffered enough in his lifetime!

Kris was at work when the call came. Impossible, she felt his death was impossible. Yes, she knew his health was fragile. It had been for many years. Erling rallied through two leg amputations, mastered an artificial limb, adapted to hand controlled vehicles, and even accepted a wheel chair. He survived by his strong determination and stubborn will. *If only, he had quit the smoking.* With a diagnosis of vascular disease, he had received strong instruction to abandon the dangerous habit. He tried several different methods for quitting but never managed it.

Too soon, he is only fifty nine years old. What happened to him? Kris felt as if the wind was knocked out of her when she got the news. Great despair and a feeling of utter panic washed over her.

Ed, their son Dean, and Kris took a couple of days to get there by car. Best, if they could stay with Ed's cousin, in Sooke. Karl and Wendy were with Ava. Upon arrival, they entered the front room, no one got up. Mom and Karl sat and stared at them with drinks in their hands. They mumbled greetings. In an atmosphere with cold body language the three newcomers sat down.

Ava began her rendition of the event, "Ja, I vas down stairs making de coffee, vaiting for him. I yelled up to him. I thought he didn't hear me. I called again, on him, from de stairvay. Ven I vent into de bedroom I vent to de vindow and said Get up. Ja, ven I turned around to his bed,

215

I knew right avay he vas gone," Ava paused, asked for another drink from Karl and continued, "I vent downstairs, drank coffee, smoked a cigarette, den I vent back up. Ja, I vashed him just like I vashed odder dead ones in de homes vere I vorked. I drank more coffee, and den I phoned."

We sat silent, listening as Ava continued.

"He knew he vas dying. Ja, I really tink he knew. Two days ago vee vent shopping. He said to me to get some food in de house. He said dat he tougt I vas getting company, not vee."

"He missed days at vork...didn't really care about driving anymore...kind of depressed, not even drinking and not eating." Karl rose from his chair, and left for the back yard. Ava went on. "Karl insists embalming for his body, s viewing of de body, dad vouldn't like dat, too much money."

"I know he did not want anything but cremation and his ashes scattered here on the island, nor does he want a service," Kris said.

"Karl said, is his turn to boss him around. He needs dis for making his good-byes."

Mother is executor and she must have agreed. It's not my turn for executorship until she has gone, thank goodness, because I would have felt the need to carry through with Erling's wishes thereby creating much discord where there is already so much.

CHAPTER 61

I must approach Karl. I must make an effort. Kris headed out to the garden thinking about the attempts, at reconciliation which failed time and again. They first met at a restaurant in Leduc, neutral territory in between their homes. Karl expressed how sorry he was for his behavior that Christmas, but then went on to lay the blame, for his anger, on Kris and Ed. His accusations flowed freely, "You pay more attention to your friends, than to me, at gatherings in your house. The truck Ed sold to me needed repairs after I bought it. You guys are Mr. and Mrs. Perfect. You guys kicked me out of your house. You don't care about me."

Kris retaliated with, "You are a part of our family, and you are more a part of hosting than being the guest in our house. I expect your part in mixing with all our friends. About the truck, it was sold in good faith without knowledge of impending problems. Have you forgotten I assumed the blame for you, smacking it up?" With your poor driving record, reporting yourself might have lost you your license and your insurance. I regret protecting you, and you say I don't care about you! We asked you to find your own place for a few different reasons. We did not kick you out, as you say. Five years, off and on, you lived with us, Karl, is that not caring? Ed helped you with work connections. I hovered over you as you lay in coma after your car accident. Took you home, nursed you along during your convalescence. We gave you notice—we did not kick you out. I don't know what you mean calling us Mr. and Mrs. Perfect. We don't say that we are."

They parted, promising each other a better time ahead. Kris felt insecure as if she lost the debate. She called Karl soon afterwards asking if they might visit him on a certain Sunday. He agreed. They called him the day before and apologized something came up. Soon after that, Kris received an intoxicated call from him. He yelled horrible accusatory insults and slammed down the phone.

I must save our relationship but how?

Kris laid a hand on his shoulder as he stood with his back to her, looking over the fence. He turned with anger on his face, "What do you want?" he demanded.

"Karl please, can't we just put our arms around each other and cry together?" With words full of venom he spat, "If you think you can use dad's death as an excuse to make up with me, think again. It won't work, get lost!"

The week got worse. They were a family, divided. Kris felt alone, somehow responsible, somehow expected to fix it. Ed was terrific in happy circumstances, capable of entertaining with jokes and silliness. He loved drawing attention to himself. Put him into a scenario such as this one and he made himself scarce. Among his excuses, Kris heard, "I don't like hospitals" and "I don't like funerals."

In her fog of grief and depression, poor choices developed for the funeral.

Everyone was ill at ease. All of them grasped at thoughts and put an itinerary together for a memorial. They sorely needed guidance. They didn't know where or who to turn to. All of them failed in part to honor Erling's wishes—no minister—no service.

The obituary included an announcement for a drop in visitation at the funeral chapel for viewing between two and three in the afternoon. It was an awkward affair.

Someone started a receiving line. Ed and Kris joined in as did Ben and Elma. Kris shook hands belonging to faces either she had forgotten or never knew. Wendy was sobbing throughout the time there. No doubt she battled her own demons since Erling kicked her out of house and home just a week prior to his death. Karl was not expected to show up. He changed his mind about wanting to see his dad. He wanted memories of him, alive. But, Karl did appear near the end. He drove his dad's car even though his license was suspended for drunk driving. He looked menacing, dressed in jeans. He avoided eye contact with everyone and stayed clear away, in a corner, by himself. Afterwards, a few people went to the pub where Erling liked to go. Others went straight to the house for sandwiches, tea and coffee, some drank alcohol. Visitors were informed the family planned on a private dinner. Karl declined. Kris' heart broke for him but she was afraid. Afraid, if she approached him once more, it might trigger another flare-up of rage.

"Kris, tomorrow vil you drive me to de crematorium and pick up de urn with Erling's ashes?" Ava asked. Kris agreed and they settled on meeting at the house at eleven the following morning. Kris drove in with jittery nerves—jittery because driving in unknown territory was scary—and jittery because she was afraid of her mother's usual temperament.

"Where is Mum?" Kris asked Karl, who reclined in Erling's chair.

"She's gone with Wendy and her friend. They're picking up Dad's ashes." Just then the car drove up and the three women came in. Ava carried the urn, waltzed over to Karl and shocked him, when she plunked the urn into his lap, "here is your dad." Without much aforethought, Kris strode right over to Karl. She took the urn into her own hands, and placed it on the cabinet, under the front room window.

"Just what am I here for, Mother? I thought you needed me to take you, and then you change your mind without letting me know."

"Vendy asked she be de one, Ja," Ava replied.

"Well, I am returning to Sooke. Auntie Lill sent an invitation to you to spend the day out there, will you come?"

"Ja dat vil be good for me, Lill is a friend to me," Ava said.

Ava was on anti-depressants and appeared drugged. The combination of pills and a couple of beers made her talkative.

"Kris, I need tell you somting, somting you don't know. I can't tell nobody ellers," she slurred.

Kris wondered with dread what was to come. "Well, tell me then."

Ava proceeded with babble of how Erling had been jealous and suspected a boyfriend in her life, and he had been unable to perform sexually for months.

"Mother for God's sake, not now. I am the wrong person. I don't want you telling me these things. This is not to talk about. Leave it between you and him."

"Dere you go again, you ja, and none of you care about me, just about him." She showed all the signs of getting out of control when dinner was announced at the right time to intervene..

Kari drove her grandmother back to Langford and dropped her off. A couple of hours passed. The phone rang, it was Karl. He requested to speak with Kris.

"I am not impressed with you at all. Mum is really upset. What the HELL went on out there?"

"Karl, you were not here, stay out of it. Don't you know mother is capable of stirring up trouble?" Kris almost collapsed, started to weep, "I can't take anymore," repeated the phrase and hung up the phone, and went straight to bed. She wept for the past, and for the future without Erling. She wept for herself, afraid of the unknown. *Just what is expected of me now?*

Later the same evening Dean called. He wanted Kris to come into Langford. Dean stayed at the house there, tagged along with Wendy and her friends, probably, they were drinking and smoking pot. "Ma, you gotta come in here. It's Granny, she's gone nuts. She sits at the kitchen table talking to Grandpa."

"Dean, I don't care. As long as she has an audience, she will perform. Ignore her, go to bed."

Back in bed Kris fumed with bad thoughts. *I wish she had died instead of Erling.* Dean called again, "Ma, you have to come. I think she over dosed on meds."

"I am not coming, those of you there, drunk or whatever, handle it yourselves. Karl, or Wendy—what about them?"

"Sleeping, Mom, sleeping, I can't wake them."

"Trust me, Dean. It will be much worse if I come, now please go to bed and take heed, don't follow in their footsteps."

Kris visualized a trip in the middle of the night. *Alone with her Mum, feed her more pills, more booze— help her to join Erling. Let him take care of her.* Her thoughts frightened her. At the time she felt capable of murder.

On the drive back home, Kris laid down on the back seat, for most of the trip. Her mind and heart was in anguished turmoil. In silence she prayed for help. *I know Ava cannot cope without Erling. I must prepare myself, be strong. I expect the worst. How will I gain peace of mind?* Kris felt alone and dwelt on the past performance and track record of her dysfunctional family. *I am gut wrenched, scared*!

CHAPTER 62

Kris chose not to burden family or friends with too much whining. She recognized the problem serious enough in her mind, and made a decision. *I must see a professional, spare my loved ones. I need my sedative prescription renewed and a referral to a psychologist.*

On her first visit she poured out words, tried telling it all. She felt release and left the office full of hope, and looked forward to the next visit.

Kris, an adult for many years now, yet the child in her, continued to crave the same love she projected to her own children. She had been told she over did it all—over protected, smothered, and was over involved—*It is my way and it helps me assuage my own need for what I missed growing up.*

After professional advice and ideas for her to practice, Kris attempted to make a few changes in her own demeanor. *I must stop acting like such a mother to everyone. I must recognize I am replaceable, and learn to receive with grace, and not always be the one to give, and know it's quite all right, not to accept bad behavior, and act strict.*

Addicted to her prescription, afraid of alcoholism she told her doctor her fears. He reassured her, "I do not believe you have the sort of personality to get hooked."

She made a conscious effort, weaned down to a smaller dose of pills, failed, and tried again.

Ava phoned, her voice slurred. Kris dreaded those calls but listened, and offered encouragement, and understanding. Kris felt like an emotional wreck when the call was over. Ava worried about her finances and Wendy's behavior. She told Kris Wendy had her friends in the house, used the beds for an orgy. Wendy sold meat from her freezer or gave it away to her friends. Wendy was always asking for money. They fought with each other. Ava now had a scar over her eye as a souvenir.

Kris suspected Wendy and Ava were drinking buddies, at Ava's expense. Wendy lived with Ava but gave nothing towards household expenses. She was often absent for days.

Each night Kris prayed, searched for guidance. A remarkable occurrence took place during just such a time. Ed was asleep beside her when 'POP' something landed on their bed, at her feet. It came as a big distraction into her thoughts, Kris investigated. A stained glass hummingbird ornament, on a suction cup hook, attached to a mirror, popped off. It cleared the dresser beneath it, travelled across the space between the dresser and the bed, and landed at Kris' feet. Remarkable, unbelievable, fixed there for a couple of years, it never came off before.

The small commotion woke Ed just enough for him to mumble, "What's going on...you okay?"

Reassuring, Kris said "Never mind, go back to sleep, I just got a message from Erling."

"Oh... good," he drifted off again.

Remembering a past conversation Kris knew that when the hummingbird took the leap Erling sent a message.

CHAPTER 63

August 28, 1990, Kris and Ed. planned for a large celebration to celebrate the success of their marriage which endured its own private pitfalls. Erling died in March of the same year. Ava came, but refused to pay Wendy's way. Inviting Karl was debatable in the first place but their thoughts went in a positive direction, just maybe, if only! He phoned our friend Marge, and in his usual loud yelling way informed her under the circumstances he definitely would not attend.

Kris made up her mind to appreciate dear friends, and other family, who were eager to help making their event a success. With Ava's presence discord between the two of them flared on the evening prior to the party.

Kris, chastised Ava, "Mother, don't start with your lamenting about anything. I don't want to hear about all your troubles, Wendy included. A lot of what is happening in your life has been brought on by yourself. You are a guest in my life this weekend, show us some respect. If you can't say anything nice about anything lease keep your mouth shut," *I wonder was it that was tough enough.*

*****

Ava called about once a week, always intoxicated, worried about the same thing as before—bills and Wendy. Kris tried to make it quite clear she could not help at this distance, "Do you want sell your home and move to Alberta?"

"I am not ready for dat," Ava replied.

Kris attended more sessions with her psychologist looking for guidance. She stopped when her yearly insurance coverage was reached.

Drunken calls came from Karl also. Always he yelled or cried. One Sunday morning after a discussion with Ed, Kris called Karl and stated, "Karl, please, we must end this painful feud. Will you try please? Listen to me, consider my suggestion—come for a visit at our cabin. I request no alcohol at all because it gets in the way and ruins everything every time. Will you agree?"

Dean and Kris picked him up at a job he was on, about an hour away on a Sunday. Karl appeared flushed and jumpy. Ed's parents were invited for dinner, helping to make Karl feel welcome with discussion about the good old days. The day passed without violence and Kris had hope—the first step towards a better relationship.

Not for long….Kris devastated again. *Why, oh why…if only!*

CHAPTER 64

Late one night, the phone rang, waking Kris from a drug induced sleep. She scrambled down the stairs in the cabin, unable to leave the phone unanswered because Ed worked away and both would worry about each other if a ringing phone was not answered. At first there wasn't anyone on the other end. Kris got no response to her greeting. She hesitated awhile, just as she was about to hang up, Karl's weak, drunken whisper entered her ear, travelled through her body—her heart skipped a beat, nausea took hold, and her knees shook.

"It's all nothing but SHIT, SHIT, and BULL SHIT," his voice ended with loud shouting. Kris visualized his spittle hitting the mouthpiece of his phone. With her head reeling and her hand tightly gripping her phone, she responded, "Karl, for God's sake, what's wrong, what's happened? Please calm down, talk to me. I don't understand." At this point, confused, not expecting anger aimed at her, Kris was close to fainting at his next outburst.

"BULL SHIT, I can't drink at your house! BULL SHIT, I can't smoke in your house, you never had asthma before, BULL SHIT!—A LOAD OF CRAP, KRIS—A LOAD OF CRAP."

"PLEASE KARL, STOP IT, STOP IT, I CAN'T TAKE THIS!" Hysterical, out of control, her tears streamed down her face, she scratched at her scalp then slammed the phone down. It rang again.

I don't want to answer but, alone in the cabin, with Ed out of town, I have to answer. If it's Ed calling he will worry about me if I don't answer. I hope it is him calling.

"What's the matter Kris? Are you upset or what, you bitch? Better watch out, I might come down there and really upset you. Maybe I'll come down and slit your throat. What's a matter? Are you scared yet?" Karl's slurred speech, varied in pitch and tone and sent chills through her.

Kris hung up again. Another call—It's Dean, not Karl.

"Hi, Ma, how's it going?"

"Oh Thank GOD, Dean, it's you," Kris told him what had just happened.

"I will call Karl and speak with him and call you back."

"Thank you, son, I love you." A few minutes later, Dean called her back.

"Ma, Karl is really sick, man, he is nutso. He needs help. He talked about getting his gun and blowing himself away."

"Dean, I will call him back and try talking sense into him. If I can't, I will contact the R.C.M.P."

Karl's voice was weak, mumbling, and incoherent but Kris made out something about blowing his brains out or coming after her. She did not hesitate. She called the Stony Plain detachment, explaining the evening's events. They promised to go to his house and to call her back.

Kris paced while she waited and watched the clock. Thirty minutes later they called.

"We went over, the house is dark and quiet, a car is on blocks in his back yard. Unless he has another vehicle, he is not on the way to your place. We will send an officer to his house in the morning. It is best not to aggravate the situation at this time. We will call and report to you tomorrow." They kept their word and contacted her the next morning.

"We have spoken with Karl. He said he suffers from depression due to the death of his father and he will get some help with it. We can't do any more but we urge you to be careful and recommend you avoid any confrontation with him whatsoever, one never knows. Maybe you might encourage him to get help. Maybe both of you should consider getting counseling."

Kris spent the next few days hiding her car in a neighbors drive way. In the fall most other cabins were empty. After work, in her spare time, Kris wrote—for companionship and therapy—adding to the story she started writing in 1986. She took an English 10 correspondence course, and passed with 72 %. Kris looked forward to a creative writing course, a fall session, at Red Deer College.

She returned to her psychologist in need of guidance once more. She came to the conclusion *counseling is necessary for more than me. One sided, counseling won't perform any magic.*

On a Sunday morning, when she thought sobriety, rather than drunkenness might greet her, she called Karl. She spoke in a gentle, comforting way, and encouraged him to consider counseling, and said without it they couldn't have a relationship. He didn't respond, grunted a little, and dismissed her call with a minor excuse. *I have put a condition on any further relationship with Karl and made it clear to him and myself, no counseling—no relationship!*

CHAPTER 65

CC had corresponded less than usual. He had been ill with cancer and suffered through surgery and convalescence. Worry for his life plagued Kris, during her quietest hours. *Am I going to lose him now, so soon?*

In one of his letters he revealed his thoughts about his close call and raised the issue of Kris' inheritance rights. CC pointed out he was after peace of mind—that the matter be settled before he died to make it easier for his wife and family. Based on his worth and as far as his calculations went, and in all fairness according to him, he offered Kris seven thousand dollars in exchange for her signature waiving her inheritance rights.

Why does this issue surface now? What is the right thing for me to do? All my life all I ever wished for from him is acknowledgment and acceptance. What answer back to him is the best answer? I do not know.

*****

Another letter arrived before she sent one back to him. He wanted to know if her step-father had adopted her. She thought he must have because she was using his last name. She asked her mother, who said yes he did but she could not produce any proof—no documents. She wrote him back with her information such as it was, and suggested CC should check Danish records.

There was no proof he informed her in the next letter and adoption would have stopped support payments.

These he paid until he was informed by Ava about her marriage. He asked if Kris received the monetary gift he had sent to Ava for their wedding gift. *I guess this gift was another not to talk about event—now I understand how Ava and Erling could afford to put on the wedding and buy us furniture*

*****

Without any more procrastination she sent her letter and her answers. She thanked him for the money he provided for their nice reception and a three room grouping of furniture. "Giving you and your family peace of mind is fine with me. Please proceed with the legalities and I will follow through with your request," she responded.

Months later Kris appeared in front of the Danish Consul in Calgary and signed the documents.

I feel strange today, as if I erased his paternity—a divorce between father and daughter. A daughter, different from his others, a threat wiped away, bribed, paid off. I am still different, I am in limbo, not adopted, but disinherited.

Kris accepted his money with tears of sadness, not with joy.

"This money is not getting invested or spent on bills," Kris said to Ed.

"I agree, whatever you want, hon."

He never pushed her one way or the other in making the decision. They purchased an oak dining room suite and front room end tables—top quality, solid oak, and custom built. Constant, durable, forever, symbols for preservation, someday heirlooms, traveling down through new generations, yet to come.

CHAPTER 66

In November of 1990, eight months after Erling passed away, another tragedy struck.

Ed and Kris were serving their guests, her bosses from work, after the Company's Christmas party. It was about an hour past midnight when the ring of the phone cut into their lighthearted conversation. Everyone looked towards the rude apparatus. Kris froze, dreading the sound of a familiar drunken voice, "Excuse me, I better answer this."

"Kris, it's Wendy...Mum's in hospital, I found her, thought she was drunk, lying on the floor. I helped her to the kitchen, to a chair. She acted weird so I called the neighbors. We got her to hospital. They say it's a stroke, what am I going to do now?" Wendy, highly intoxicated, sounded as though she bordered on hysteria.

"Please calm down and tell me again, when did this happen?"

"I found Mum earlier in the day," Wendy slurred.

"Why did you wait so long to call?"

"It was dad's Christmas staff party tonight, I went in Mum's place—she's in hospital, Dad's dead, Mum was invited." Wendy babbled.

Kris lost her patience with Wendy and bawled her out for acting garish. "Decent people don't go partying under such circumstance, a sober call to me when first it happened, instead of a drunken one at this hour would have been much more appropriate and appreciated."

Wendy yelled and cursed at Kris.

"Calm down, sleep it off. I will talk to you tomorrow."

CHAPTER 67

Plans were under way for Ed's parents' fiftieth wedding anniversary. Their airline tickets were already purchased. Ann and Al looked forward to their three children plus spouses arriving in Mesa, Arizona for their important occasion.

Not without guilt, Kris decided to carry on as planned, knowing full well she must soon face up to the responsibility of handling whatever is left, of her mother's life. In the meantime Ava was under hospital care, receiving therapy, weaning off alcohol, and with any luck, reaching some sort of decision on her own as to her future. Kris was able to put Ava's affairs on the back burner for a few weeks at least. Karl was flying out there during December, staying until after Christmas. Kris remembered her counseling and told her-self the world would go on without her. She let go—for a short time.

Fast asleep at Aunt Jeans' place, just a block away from Ann and Al's—they resided in the same retirement park—Kris heard the phone ringing.

She picked up the receiver and then heard Ann's voice, "Kris, I just gave Karl the phone number. I think he plans to call you right away...I'm sorry but he was upset. I don't know if anything happened to Ava." Karl's call came right after Kris disconnected from Ann. It was not a sober call.

"Kris things are bad out here. I'm having a bad time of it. I kicked Wendy out of the house. Mum was home for Christmas and I had to help her on the toilet, and pull her pants up. I CAN'T DO THIS ANYMORE, IT'S NOT MY JOB! IT'S YOUR JOB AND WHERE THE HELL ARE YOU? IN ARIZONA AT A PARTY! SHE'S YOUR MOTHER FOR CHRIST'S SAKE. YOU SHOULD BE HERE!"

Kris did not interrupt his tirade. She waited until he halted, "Karl may I remind you she is your mother too. I know well enough I have a job ahead of me, in the meantime, sink or swim as you choose. Right now I have a job here, a pleasant one of course. I am sticking with this one until it's done."

"When Dad had his heart attack you wasted no time getting to his bed-side. This is no different. Why aren't you here now with Mum?"

Kris hesitated. *Here's an invitation to a guilt trip. It's up to me whether I take the trip or not.* "THAT was then and THIS is now and I will not discuss it anymore. I will let my plans be known when I know what they will be. Good night Karl." She set the phone gently in its cradle and heard he slammed his.

*****

Kari returned to Victoria University after the holidays, and moved into her grandmother's home at Kris 'request. Unoccupied it was an invitation for break and enters by the known or unknown culprits.

A few days later Kari called, "Mom, I am uncomfortable here. Karl left the house in a mess—dirty dishes in the sink, coffee and grounds in the coffee maker gone moldy, and every ash tray over flowing. There was even stinking rotting garbage left in the can."

"I'm sorry Kari. I hope you'll be all right there until I get there. I gave two weeks of notice at work. I quit. They offered me a leave of absence but I think I cannot cope with the pressures—moving mother to Alberta, selling her house, and all the rest of it."

After their discussion, Kris' thoughts drifted back in time, remembering Ava's abortion wish. Now, this granddaughter of hers, helping out, visiting her in hospital, treating her with kindness. A few short months ago, Kari had taken her on a trip to Oregon. *I wonder if mother has ever given her abortion wish for me a thought.*

The first thing on Kris' agenda after her arrival in Victoria was taking care of finances. She began by breaking the lock on the kitchen drawer which held important papers, and she couldn't find a key for it anywhere. The contents of the drawer were not in any order. The documents revealed hard evidence of the chaos of her parents' lives for quite a long while. No longer is she the youngster, snoopy and sneaky, going through papers hoping to find answers to her questions. Now, she is the grownup, taking charge, setting things in order, and a detective, shocked at the revelation...

Bank statements, canceled checks, and utility bills fanned out, entwined on the top. After sorting these into order by date and setting them neatly aside, Kris dug deeper into the paper pile. Hunched over the drawer, sitting on a kitchen chair, on her mind is Erling's and Ava's past year or so—a vivid play.

Court documents and correspondence from lawyers are the script. Months before Erling's death, a charge of impaired driving against him supported the lawyer bills and fines coming to a whopping four thousand bucks. It was obvious he had spent the money, hoping he'd get off– –not so. Now she understood why he did not drive when they last visited.

There was a charge of impaired driving causing property damage, against Ava, but there was a letter stating Erling had done the deed, signed by him.

Another letter, this one from a different lawyer revealed this case was not yet settled. Ava was still in big trouble over this. She had driven her car through someone's house.

"Oh, my God," Kris said out loud to herself. "What a mess!"

There were utility bills due. She worked with the bank statements, checking off the canceled checks. One was made out to Wendy, for two hundred dollars, dated a couple of days after Ava's stroke. *This signature is definitely not Ava's. How will all this end?* Kris' first day was over, she headed off to bed.

Karl had taken the car home with him and Kari drove hers to the university. Without a vehicle, Kris took public transit to the hospital and didn't mind it. She found the walk, before and after, and the ride itself, allowed her time to get in touch with her soul, prepare to cope.

*****

Kris hesitated in the doorway leading into her mother's room. Kris observed her for a few seconds before Ava saw her. Ava looked listless, hopeless, to Kris.

"Hi, there, I'm here," Kris announced with false cheerfulness.

Ava struggled for control, gasped and choked on her sobs.

Sympathy, pity, and other unknown emotions overwhelmed Kris, and she too choked on her own crying.

Kris bent over Ava's reddening face. Tears pushed against her eyelids, the tears released. She placed her hand on Ava's. Awkward, she attempted an embrace and said "I am going to help, don't worry, everything will turn out okay." It was a one sided embrace—no gesture, no word, no light in Ava's eyes.

Dejected, Kris straightened up and pulled back. She realized Ava's sobbing was self-pity.

"Well, Mum, It is a difficult time and we will figure out what needs doing considering your present state of health. First, let's tour this nice place, inside and out." As Kris helped her into a wheel chair she observed her handicap. Her left arm was limp, as limp as can be. It hung, supported in a sling. Her fingers were curled into a frozen grip. Ava's left leg was somewhat functional, in a dragging, weak manner. The left side of her face drooped a little. Kris listened to Ava's speech as she told Kris about the extended care facility. Kris didn't pick up on any speech impediment.

"See dat guy over dere in de electric vheel chair, Ja, de guy with de black cap on his head? Dat's de guy Vendy got in an accident vit."

I wonder did I forget something I think I was never told about before. "Tell me Mum, what actually happened?"

"Vendy got de job, Ja, living in, looking after him, you know?"

"Do you mean his personal assistant?"

"Ja, dat's right and he ovned a handicap van vit a lift dat Vendy drove him around in. One day after drinking together, Vendy drove, got in an accident. Ja, he got hurt, end of dat job. Now, he lives here."

"Speaking of Wendy, Mum, do you still support her, you know, give her money?"

"No more, no more! I don't know vat to do vit dat girl. Dad told her, get out, just before he died and Karl told her, get out, ven he got here at Christmas. She visited me just once ven I first got in here."

"Did she ask you for money then?"

"No."

"Mum, where is your check book? I am taking charge of your affairs and need to pay bills and I must know how much money you have. Tomorrow I am seeing the lawyer who helped you and dad with your wills and activate my Power of Attorney." Ava produced her check book from her purse. Kris noticed the number on the top check, and knew right then, Wendy plucked out the preceding one and forged Ava's signature.

*****

The lawyer delivered a lecture, such as should be given to persons of questionable character. She disliked him, he offended her. The lecture was about her responsibility, her liability, and her accountability. *The lawyer does not know me but still I feel insulted.* She took her leave. *If only, he knew...*

Armed with legal papers, she went about the business of organizing, and completing affairs. Erling's final income tax still needed filing and the closing of a bank account, with little money in it, but still in his name.

When Kris knew the house mortgage, pay-out, she met with a realtor for discussion about selling the town house. Before proceeding with anything else, she had to find out about her mother's prognosis for recovery. Where will her best place of residence be and just how much of her stuff would she still need?

She made an appointment with a rehabilitation counselor at the extended care facility. It turned into a major outpouring of Kris' emotions concerning the dysfunctional family including the excessive drinking habits and the lack of communications. Kris spoke of her willingness to help Ava move to Alberta but not without conditions attached. As far as Ava's recovery from the stroke, Kris learned it was unpredictable, each stroke victim was different. The councilor promised a session with Ava alone and then a session with both of them.

*****

She packed and visualized how it seemed to her Ava's life should turn out in the future. Kris made a long list of duties for herself to accomplish. *Keep enough for a one bedroom apartment-—the newest and the oldest of possessions—furnishings and heirlooms. A garage sale seems a great idea. Turn things into cash to help offset moving costs.*

Kris raked up leaves from the grass and spruced up the appearance of the place insuring it would show well to perspective buyers. She was at the raking when Wendy popped by wanting information about the plans for Ava.

"I was goanna do the raking here but, then I don't live here anymore, too bad."

"Yes Wendy, it's all too bad and too bad you don't even visit your mother in the hospital and too bad you stole money from her. I saw the forged check. That's appalling."

"Kris, I was desperate. I had no money. I haven't any transportation to and from the hospital. You just don't understand!"

"No, I guess I don't and you know what? I don't plan to worry about you anymore. I can't help you for you won't help yourself. You're on your own. Mum is the only one I can help now."

"Several things here belong to me and I want them."

"I don't have a problem with that. Take them today and then before the yard sale, you may come and see what else you want. I'll talk to Mum about all her possessions before they are given away or sold. By the way, Wendy, I'm arranging for the handy-van to bring her home for a visit overnight next weekend. If you want to see her, come then.

"Well, I'll try, gotta go, bye." Wendy walked away. Kris leaned on the rake, wanted it to feel alive, warm and comforting. Soon her thoughts returned to the task at hand but her mind wandered, going to her 'if only' thoughts."

CHAPTER 68

Karl had brought Mum's bed downstairs at Christmas time and it stood in the front room. With a half bath on the main floor Ava managed with minimal help. Ava put in her request for Danish meatballs and some of her other favorites.

Kris didn't mind the cooking at all, as long as she could fit in a chat session regarding Ava's possessions.

Maintaining a positive attitude, regarding this as the adventure, for a new beginning was easy for Kris. She pretended to be in Ava's place. Soon, Kris was reminded her mother and she were different in many ways. Kris saw Ava's inner thoughts were still dark and gloomy, and self-pitying. Some things about her were different. Ava did not rant out loud, didn't huff and puff as if possessed by a threatening monster. She did not stomp from room to room because of course she was not able to. She sulked, stared, and seemed unaware of what was going on around her. Deep loud sighing, was her new way to get attention.

Kari and Kris tried making conversations with her. Ava answered either "Oh, Ja" or with a plain "no." It seemed full sentences were locked up inside of her.

At meal time she displayed bad table manners, reached out for food before anyone else sat down, ate fast, then showed impatience while she waited for Kris to light her cigarette.

Kris hauled Ava's entire closet contents down into the living room and displayed them in front of Ava. Going through the elimination process Kris came to her senses—this was a bad idea. Ava wanted to keep high heeled shoes not worn in ten years and dresses too difficult for her to maneuver into. Kris just nodded, but knew she would make the decision on her own and sort after Ava was returned to the hospital.

Grasping for quality time together, Kris decided to look through the photos in Ava's albums and those lying loose in shoe boxes. Kari started with an album and Kris headed for the kitchen to prepare a snack. "Vere is my odder daughter?" Ava asked.

"They are there, Kris and Wendy."

"No...My odder daughter," Ava sounded frustrated.

Kari came around the corner into the kitchen with a puzzled frown on her face, "Mom, did you hear?"

242

"I did and don't ask me what's going on," Kris went to her mother's side and asked "Do you mean where Karl is or maybe where is Kaj?"

"No, I mean my odder daughter, you know."

"No mother, I don't know, might you be thinking of one of your sisters?"

"No." Ava's lips clamped tight.

I will ask the councilor at the hospital about this incident for sure. I wonder if there existed yet another secret or was my mother acting out for attention.

Sunday afternoon, before the arrival of the handy-van, Kris announced Mum should prepare, get ready and be waiting, not to hold up its schedule. Ava begun sniffling, and then broke into a sob, "vhy do I have to stay in hospital? I don't even know vhy I'm in dere anyvay!"

Sympathetic but emphatic, Kris reminded her about physiotherapy and the difficulty of a prolonged stay in her own home. She promised her more short visits home, later. Kris welcomed the sight of the van and rejoiced as it drove away with Ava.

*****

The house sold quickly, and the paper work was easy and unobstructed. Ed's relatives, Uncle Ed and Aunt Ilene were visiting relatives in Sooke. Aunt Ilene helped Kris with the pricing and displaying of garage sale items.

Ava was turning 66 years old, and plans got under way for a small party in her honor. She came home again, for the last time. Wendy showed up in tight pink spandex and black leather. The living room was filled with boxes

Kris had sorted and packed. The movers had brought her the boxes and they would pick them up full. The moving van was due to arrive in Alberta after Kris took the flight home. The cost of moving was a lot more than the yard sale netted—a meager profit of $169.00, not worth the time or trouble to organize it.

Kris visited Ava at the hospital one last time. They were scheduled for a counseling appointment together. The room was small, crowded with three people in it. The councilor sat behind a large desk, Ava was in her wheel chair and Kris was right beside her. There was a window beside Ava. Most of the time, Ava craned her neck towards the outside. The councilor broached all the subjects Kris had confided to her before—Ava's alcohol abuse, her current legal problem regarding her driving into a house and the impaired charge against her. Does Ava want a move to Alberta or does she want to stay in Victoria?

Ava's answers were short and sharp. She appeared ill at ease. She denied her drinking problem, threw Kris a venomous glare, tears fell from her eyes filled with hate. Kris extended her hand out taking Ava's hand in hers.

Ava wrenched it away roughly, turning back towards the window. The councilor reached for the call button on her intercom and requested a porter come and transport Ava back to her room.

Kris' tears fell into her hands. Kris was given a tissue followed by the cold hard facts.

"Ava is a private individual with a lot buried deep inside her. She is unable to show you any love or affection of any kind. Too much time has passed. It is much too late to hope for anything more. If you can't help her, knowing she will remain this way, then leave her here."

"I wouldn't respect myself nor could I endure my guilty conscience if I don't help her and move her to Alberta. If she stays here, who will care...Not Wendy for sure! I am not offering out of love but simple respect for humanity. My mother made sure I was clothed, was warm and was fed, when I was a child. I am able to give at least that much back. I'll protect her finances, see her bills are paid and include her in family get-togethers. She is not going to live in my home because there I draw the line. I will apply to a care facility nearby."

Kris received advice on such an application and the medical staff there would draft a letter to the courts verifying Ava's disability, asking for lenient consideration on her impending impaired charge.

Kris flew home and Aunt Elma drove down from Nanaimo and escorted Ava to her court appearance where she was asked to hand over her drivers' license promising never to drive again. Elma helped again when she put Ava on a plane three months later.

She was accepted into the Red Deer Nursing Home, in Alberta.

CHAPTER 69

Ava seemed nervous and agitated when Kris collected her at the airport. Travel on a plane, alone, and with her mobility problem, would scare anyone, Kris thought. She drove Ava straight to the nursing home. They expected her. Kris had attended a familiarizing session a few days before and now knew her way about and all the rules and schedules. The contact person in Red Deer in charge of placement worked quickly processing Ava's application. Kris broke down in her office at talk of their family tale. It must have touched her for she sent Kris a cheery note. Kris was introducing Ava to the charge nurse when Ava began a gut deep sobbing. The nurse hugged her and spoke kind and soft words to her.

Mother didn't wrench away from the nurse. She lapped up the kindness. Kris did not attempt any consoling. *I must look the cold uncaring daughter.* Kris took her leave as soon as possible, "I will return tomorrow to pick Mum up for a visit to our cabin," she told the nurse.

Ava's first room was undesirable and so were the different roommates. She moved through the system, first a semi private room then a private, bright one came available. Kris decorated her space with Ava's own familiar belongings. At the same time she encouraged her mother to accompany her to various senior lodges and apartments around Red Deer.

"If, she sees something she likes then maybe she will try harder, aim for a more productive and independent life for herself," Kris explained to Ed. Soon it was evident to Kris these were her own dreams, not Ava's.

One afternoon at a Stroke Support Group meeting––also Kris' idea they join the group—the agenda was games, puzzles or just visiting amongst members. Ava turned down invitations for any involvement, giving only her short usual answer, "No."

Kris picked a table of scrabble players and encouraged Ava to play along as her helper.

Ava just stared with a blank expression, she started to fidget, "take me out for a smoke."

It was cold, wet, and blowing outside. Kris shivered, watched Ava wrapped in a blanket, and sitting on a thick warm cushion in her wheel chair, sucking in, blowing out.

The thought came clear and cleansing for Kris. "Let's go Mum. You aren't enjoying this anyway are you?"

"No...Not really."

Kris gave her a calendar, marked the meeting dates and time of functions. She gave her Handy-van tickets along with their phone number for her to make her own reservations. Kris never attended another outing with the stroke support group.

Ava did bond with one woman, Effie, in the smoking room of the nursing home.

"Oh, ja, hi, push me in for a smoke," Ava said the same as always. Kris refused to sit in the smoking room for long, and her visits to Ava were quite short

On most Sundays, someone picked Ava up and brought her to Ed and Kris' home, for the day. Mid-week Kris either took her shopping or dropped off her things—a carton of cigarettes, all the gossip magazines, and her sweets. Ava demanded no more and seemed content.

Gone was Kris' nervousness around her mother and their relationship was more bearable, for the first time Kris could recall.

Ava loved the attention Ed dished out to her. He would tease, and joke around with her. She smiled a crooked small smile and acted bashful around him

*****.

Since Ava now resided in Alberta, Kris wanted her legal affairs in proper order. She made an appointment with an attorney. Ava's assets were to be divided at the time of her death between her surviving children. Kris was appointed executor and in the meantime she had power of attorney. Kris consulted with her mother every month regarding her expenses and bank balance. She brought checks to Ava for her signature in an attempt to keep her involved and interested, a useless attempt. Erling handled their financial affairs and Ava preferred living in La-La land.

With Kris' name on Ava's bank account, the routine was to bring in Ava's bank statements every few months.

Ava glanced at them with disinterest, "I'm doing OK aren't I?" was Ava's usual question. Kris reassured her, often encouraged her to spend money perhaps on a small refrigerator and an easy chair designed to stand her up by the push of a button.

"No, not yet, ja, I have no need for dem."

CHAPTER 70

The thought of travel appealed to Ava and Kris accompanied her to Dartmouth that summer. They enjoyed a trip to Prince Edward Island in a rented van. Kris plotted—encouraged her Mother to tell stories of her childhood, one evening in a motel, "you know mother, your grandkids know little of their Danish heritage and I don't know much about your childhood. Please tell stories. What was it like when you were a girl in Denmark?"

"It vas Okay."

"How about your real dad, he died when you were quite young? Tell me about him."

"Noting to tell, ja, I don't remember much. Dis is silly, get me a smoke!" They enjoyed sightseeing and eating sea food. They saw the play 'Anne of Green Gables' in Charlottetown and visited the famous green house on P.E.I. Ava was disappointed, to learn that 'Anne and Gilbert' were fictional characters. She had watched the series on her television and believed it was based on a true story.

CHAPTER 71

Often, Kris received phone calls from Karl, asking how Ava was doing and giving excuses for his infrequent visits. A call from him was always unpleasant. Karl reminded Kris not to go on a power trip, handling their mother's affairs. He planned to scrutinize her accounting. Kris took offense, felt hurt Karl harbored a need to insult her that way. "I didn't ask or fight for the job, but, now it is my job and you have just given me a vote of non-confidence. You, don't have much faith in me, why?" He hung up the phone. *I feel apart, different, removed. I would not trust him with the job!*

Ed and Kris were making a change in residence. "Ed, I won't be giving Karl the directions to our new house. I am glad it's a rural address and it won't be published in any phone book. He scares me."

"I agree, he is very unstable, and he is not welcome in our house anymore."

They sold their condo and cabin. The new house was ready for occupancy on Christmas day 1991. They had it built wheel chair friendly and expected to have many years of entertaining family and friends.

*****

In October of 1991 Kris was amazed at the emotion shown by Ava. This was the prestigious visit by Queen Margrethe of Denmark at the Dickson Store Museum. Mum sat in her wheel chair, along with other senior Danish immigrants, right in front of Queen Margrete and Prince Hendrik. Queen Margrete shook hands with those up front. Kris missed capturing it on both picture and video. She was at the back fighting the crowd for a chance to videotape the event. Ava trembled with tears after the hand shake. *If I were the queen of Denmark maybe then she might show emotion for me.*

250

"Ja, Kris I vish I could make one more visit to Danmark. Ja, dat is not possible,"

"Well you have enough money to go but not alone, you need too much assistance,"

"Do I have enough to pay, for two to go?"

"I think you do, who do you want to take you?"

"Vil you come, ja, will Ed let you take me?"

"Mum, I have an idea. It would be nice if two people went. I will have support and help with luggage, and more. Can you understand?"

"Ja, vel I vil not pay for two and who ellers should come?"

"I would love to take Kari when she finishes her classes this spring. If we each paid for half our ticket and you paid the other half, it's still affordable."

"Ja, dat is nice." Kris felt happy and excited about asking Kari.

"Wow, Mom super, are you sure Granny will pay half for us?"

"I am sure of it and when I mentioned your name her eyes lit up."

Away they went on economy tickets and by sheer luck they were placed in first class both ways.

"Mum there is something I must say before we arrive in Denmark. I plan to visit with my father and his family and to introduce Kari to her biological grandfather. You will not be included."

"Ja, okay, I don care!"

CHAPTER 72
DENMARK

Kris was grateful Kari came. It took two of them at Ava's bath or shower time.

A good time and many good memories came out of the trip. Kris' highlight was again greeting CC and his family who held a family dinner.

One afternoon he asked Kris to take a walking tour around Ribe town. CC pointed out many buildings and explained their history and spoke of the people who once occupied them. "Oh, hello, Mrs. Sorensen, I see you still enjoy riding your bike on a nice day," CC addressed an older woman who stopped her bike alongside them.

"Why, if it isn't, CC out strolling and with a pretty young lady for company. What does Ruth have to say?" asked the nosy woman.

"Let me introduce you to Kirsten, my daughter. I had her before I was married."

"Good day, Mrs. Sorensen, nice to make your acquaintance," Kirsten gave a little curtsy making sure to impress the lady who just heard the best gossip in a long while and would hurry to find persons to share it with. *He talked about me without shame. Wow!*

"Good Day, to both of you. I better get cycling and get my errands done."

CC showed Kris the white board house across from Ribe Domkirke—the house in which he was born. He pointed at an upstairs window, "That is the bedroom I shared with my brother. I was fourteen, he was eighteen, the night German Gestapo invaded our home, took him away because of his involvement with the underground during WWII. They put him in a concentration camp. He came home after the end of the war sick and undernourished, and he died three months later. I have always missed him. Come, I will show the memorial stone over by St. Katrina Church square. It has names on it in recognition for bravery. His name is one of them."

Kris went for afternoon tea at his home and CC showed his brother's letters, to her. They were all stamped GESTAPO in bright red.

"He lied about healthy food, fresh air and lots of exercise, and of general good treatment. Otherwise his letters would not have come through, letting the family know he was alive," CC told her.

Kari was impressed with the family get together, meeting her maternal grandfather and his family. They had many good times too with Ava's side—many loving relatives.

CHAPTER 73
CANADA

In the summer of 1992, relatives would be coming from Denmark. *Hurrah! Hurrah! A treat for all, a welcome joy!*

Ava's sister, Inger, her daughter and Kris' childhood play-mate, Nita, and Claus, Nita's son, would be guests for a few weeks. It was a special time for Nita, who was off kidney dialysis, after several years. Nita and Inger were both post-op from a mother, daughter, kidney donation and transplant. Two years earlier, Nita received a cadaver kidney donation but it failed. Nita almost died from infection and complications.

The house was filled. Kari flew home from Victoria for a weekend. Ed's parents lived nearby. They loaned the group their car for a mountain excursion and a trip to the Tyrell museum in Drumheller. Ava was out of the nursing home a lot and enjoyed all the excitement with her sister and niece paying her a lot of attention.

Wendy and her on-again, off-again husband, Don arrived for a visit. They met at a horse ranch where a wiener roast and hayride were planned. We didn't plan to include alcohol but Wendy, off and on, walked over to their vehicle. She became intoxicated and sloppy. They travelled with Wendy's little dog, it got fed whatever was lying around. Don was not as drunk. After the hayride everyone met back at Ed and Kris' house.

"Don and Wendy, I can recommend a motel nearby for you guys for tonight as we are full house. You are welcome to come back in the morning for breakfast," Kris stated.

I can't feel hospitality towards them, not even floor space for sleeping. I feel familiar nervousness of impending behavior problems.

Wendy was about to answer when the dog vomited on the deck. *Thank goodness, not inside on my white carpet.* "Wendy, please keep the dog out here."

After breakfast, they took their leave with things Ava agreed to part with. Away with them went the tension Kris felt.

Karl wanted to visit with the relatives. He picked them and Ava up at the nursing home and dropped them off there again because Karl and Kris didn't see each other anymore. Kris made a strict decision and informed Karl of it. Unable to patch things up, and because Karl would not attend counseling, Kris was at last able to practice tough love.

CHAPTER 74

The relationship between Kris and Ava and their routine settled into a manner Kris had established to suit her. She was now the controlling one and Ava was dependent on her for contact outside the nursing home. Ava had stopped complaining.

On a sunny morning in July, Kris answered the telephone, "Hello"

"Hi, I am calling from the Red Deer Nursing Home, is this Kirsten?"

"Yes, this is Kirsten, how may I help you?"

"Your Mother has not felt well through the night and this morning, perhaps you should pay her a visit right away."

"I will be there soon as I can. Thank you for calling."

"Mum, what is wrong? I got a call—said I should come?"

"I don't know, maybe a flu bug, I vomit and diarrhea all night long, tired."

"Well, you rest. I am going for groceries. I will check in later. Do you need anything in the way of cigarettes, chocolates, magazines, or mints?"

"No, no, just go."

Kris did her shopping, went home, put them away, and decided to take a bath before going back to visit Ava. The phone rang as she toweled off.

"Hi, Kirsten, it's about your mother, we called for an ambulance and she is at the hospital."

"What? I saw her this morning and was just about to come again."

"Well, dear, then I caught you in time. You best head to the hospital."

"Yes, of course I will. Thank you for calling."

When Kris entered Ava's room she found her mother all tucked in looking comfortable with a drip in her arm.

"Mum, what does the doctor say is wrong, is it another stroke?"

"No, is congestive heart failure. I don't understand. Never anyting wrong with my heart before."

"Well, they are treating it quite serious. Do you know you are in the intensive care ward?"

"No, but I sure am goanna miss smoking with Effie ven I get back to de home. Look at dis book on dangers of smoking and how to quit."

256

"Do you think you will manage to quit?"

"I have to, ellers I vil die. I need a new bat robe, a varm one for here so go buy one. Give you somting to do. Bring it tomorrow. You better go, ja, I am tired."

"Do you want me to phone, Karl?"

"Ja, you better, ellers he will get mad at you. He don't have to come, tell him dat."

"Okay then, I am off. Behave yourself, no smoking remember. See you tomorrow."

No hugs, no touching—neither one would have felt comfortable.

"Karl, this is Kris. I am letting you know Mum is in the hospital in Red Deer."

"Why?"

"To do with her heart, I haven't had a chance to talk to a doctor. But, she is in intensive care."

"Should I come see her?"

"Your choice, not for me to say, Mum said I should tell you it was not necessary."

"Okay I will think about it."

Kris hung up the phone just as it started to ring, "Hello Kirsten, this is the hospital calling. We need to know about resuscitation for Ava."

"Is she really that ill?"

"We can't control her levels, it is serious. We asked her but she has confusion about it. She seems to thinks she wants it, what do you know?"

"Please call the Red Deer Nursing Home. They have her request on file. When they held the meeting with the doctor and staff there, I asked to be excused and left the room when the question came up. I did not want to influence her decision. I think it will say no resuscitation!"

"Karl this is Kris again. I thought I should let you know Mum's condition is serious."

Kris explained about the resuscitation inquiry. She told him she was pretty sure there would be no resuscitation.

"What the hell, I want everything done to keep her alive. You bitch, you want to kill her. Well we will see, I will be coming down there and make sure they do all they can."

"Karl, it's not your choice. Don't be coming down here with thought of creating a scene."

Kris and Ed were eating their evening meal with plans to visit Ava afterwards. Their meal was interrupted by the phone. It was the hospital and Ava's condition was grave—they should come right away.

They were too late. Ava passed July 20, 1994. Kris stood beside her mother's body and took her hand in hers, "Mum, this is one time you will not pull away from me. You have passed on, my life, as it has been from the start to now will be different. With you at peace in death, I pray for peace in my life. Good bye, Mother."

A nurse entered the room, "I am sorry for your loss. How are you doing?"

Kris' eyes were dry, "I am okay."

"Your brother Karl was here. He created quite a commotion. He was drunk, we called security. They forced him to go outside."

"Did he speak with Ava before she died?"

"He was with her only for a short while."

A booming, cursing, and drunken voice broke into the quiet surroundings.

"I am reporting this place. Who built this God damn place? I get lost. Wait till I get my hands on the bitch of a sister. She is a killer."

"Please excuse me. I can't let him see me. I have to run, it won't be pretty," Kris' voice quavered.

"Hurry, please leave, we will get security again."

"I will contact Red Deer Funeral Home. Thank you!"

She managed to leave before a confrontation happened with Karl. Kris called Wendy to tell her Mum died. Kris shed tears later in private. She cried for what she and her mother never had.

No funeral, no memorial, Kris and family attended the cremation. Ava's ashes were left with the funeral home. Karl picked them up and he would spread them in BC, the same place as Erling's ashes. Wendy went with him.

CHAPTER 75

Ed's mother, Ann, was in the hospital at the same time Ava was. She was battling cancer for more than 2 years. Ed's dad passed away the year before. He had prostate cancer which seemed to respond well to treatment. But, he developed acute aggressive leukemia. It was a big shock to the family, when he passed.

Kris spent many hours by Ann's bedside. She hoped to be there for her so she would not die alone. Ann passed away five months after Ava in December of 1994. There was a large memorial with lots of loving friends and family.

During Kris' time sitting beside Ann's death bed, she composed a letter to her dear departed Bedstemor. The creative writing class she attended suggested this approach as one way to break a writer's block.

Dear Bedste;

November 14, 1994

I think of you often, especially when times are tough for me. I think of how you may have reacted in situations such as I am faced with. These last few years have been difficult. Just now my mother-in-law is lying at death's door. She has surpassed many, life threatening moments in the past two years, baffling medical staff as well as family and friends.

Bedste—this morning I lay in bed, thinking of three women who have had such an impact on my life. You, first of all, the one I have always tried to clone myself after, secondly, my mother, the one I want to be least like, last but not least, my mother-in-law. An awakening comes to me as I realize it is with my mother-in-law, Ann, I have spent more time than with the two of you. Of her traits, I wish to pick and choose, keeping all I admire about her and discarding the characteristics of hers which annoyed me.

Bedste—I don't remember any single negative thing about you. I remember love, fun, and friendship. Mother has been gone these past three months I reflect back—how she mellowed since her stroke. I realise she became a different person the last four years. I am more comfortable remembering her that way than the way she was before. You remember too how she was, don't you? You and I talked about it, neither one of us able to understand her.

Bedste—do souls really re-unite in the hereafter? Have you and mother run into each other? I know you met Ann only once, therefore I wonder if you will recognise her if you do meet again, wherever this might be. When my turn comes will we know each other again? My thoughts now turn to my daughter.

Bedste—you saw her only once when she was three years old. I want you to know there's a lot of you in her. She has grown to be a wonderful person and I tell you my time is well spent, cultivating our relationship. Your great-grand daughter is about to advance, promoted in the ranks of generations. I trust she carries the best of traits from the women she has learned from and some day she is going to play an important part influencing her future children. If all goes well...

Bedste—I might become a grandmother in 1996. Thanks to you, I am not afraid to face this new role. I will truly practice being just like you.

Bedste—I thank you for the memory of you, comforting to me until we meet again.
With love, your barnebarn, Kirsten Marie

CHAPTER 76

Life was good without too much stress. Kris became a grandmother to Mackenzie in early 1997. She wrapped herself into the loving role she had visualized many times before. Kris and Ed moved to be closer and Kris was in love with her surroundings and the people she spent time with.

Once in a while, a disturbing derogatory drunken phone call would come from Karl. They could not change their phone number due to Ed's business or they would have. Kris continued to practice tough love.

"Listen up, Karl. If you call me, and I hear you are drunk, I will hang up. Call me when you are sober and we will talk but remember no counseling, no contact."

Wendy called a few times and her calls were about as bad as Karl's and Kris gave her the same spiel. One evening when Kris was in bed the phone rang, "Hi, Kris, this is Marion, your cousin."

"Well hello, I have not spoken with you in a long while, how are you?"

"I am sorry but I have bad news. Wendy called me…Karl is dead. He shot himself. His girlfriend called Wendy."

"Oh My God, I don't know what to say. I don't know what to do. Marion, what are the details?"

"I don't know. Wendy was hysterical on the phone, hard to understand."

"Okay, bye, for now." Kris tossed and turned all night. She called the Stony Plain RCMP the next day. They referred her to Victim Services.

"Hello, my name is Kirsten. I am calling regarding my brother Karl, age 43, who committed suicide according to what a relative told me. We have been estranged for many years and I am lost as to what I should do. What is expected of me?"

"Kirsten, first I must tell you Karl and his common law wife were well known to the police. There have been many calls about domestic violence, complaint calls from their neighbors. This morning, RCMP was called by the funeral home. When your sister Wendy arrived there and asked to see his body, she threw herself on top of the body, screaming. No one could calm her. She struck out at the staff. When the police arrived they had to drag her. She clung to the sheet and as a result the body landed on the floor."

"This is indicative of my family and is why I chose to keep them away from me and mine. As his sister, am I bound by any reason to involve myself?"

"No, you are not. I will tell you what we have determined. Karl was drunk, on muscle relaxing pills for his sore back and he argued with his girlfriend. Whatever the topic was is not clear but it is reported he pulled a .22 caliber gun and said "You think that's bad, just watch this." He then put the gun against his forehead and pulled the trigger!

Kris began sobbing, "My once sweet little brother. How did this come to be? I am sorry for crying. This is just awful!"

The kind stranger on the phone said, "Take care of yourself, my dear."

I am in for a circus show if I go there or attend his funeral." Kris did not attend.

She planted two long rows of hedge on the day of Karl's funeral—Caragana, fast growing, full of buzzing wasps—Lilacs sweet, pretty for a short time. August 1997 a sad year, Princess Diana died a week later.

CHAPTER 77
DENMARK

In 2003, Kris travelled to Denmark alone. She stayed with Aunt Inger, Ava's sister, and Uncle Soren for a week in Ribe. She travelled to Copenhagen and stayed with Aunt Asta, also Ava's sister, and Uncle Manfred. She met with quite a few cousins and enjoyed the sane and loving family.

A highlight was when CC and Ruth invited her to stay with them as their guest in the small private suite in their house.

Fifty four years old and I am sleeping under my father's roof. I recall my many fantasies and my 'if only' thoughts. There are angels to help with the thoughts one puts out there. I will always thank them for the miracles I have received."

Kris thought of this visit as her special bonding time with Ruth. The atmosphere was congenial, warm, and cozy.

If I could have lived with them here, then Ruth would have been the sweet mother. Stop fantasizing. Stop 'if only' thoughts. Be happy, love Ruth, and thank my Angels for bringing her into my life.

"Kirsten, there is something I want to say, something I need to say. Please forgive me for standing between you and your father in the past. I was a silly, jealous woman. Now I know you, I love you and you must always be a part of our family." They stood facing each other, holding hands. Kris embraced Ruth who wrapped her arms around Kris. They shared tears, then smiles.

"Of course I forgive you. I understand how you must have felt. You are a gracious and special person and I am grateful you have been in my father's life, loving him with all the warmth you have in your heart. I feel your warmth and I love you, too."

CHAPTER 78
CANADA

Kris returned home to Canada to family including two grandkids, Emma and Mackenzie, always happy to see her. They greeted her with open arms, and right away asked for her to tell them stories.

Living near Rocky Mountain House, in the bush they all called it. Separate dwellings but next door, to those precious children, Kris was happier than ever. She appreciated the tranquility of nature. She loved sitting in a rocking chair, by the window, with baby Emma in her arms, watching deer that frequented the property.

Nothing stayed the same, Kari and Tim bought a business in BC. The property was sold. Kris mourned. *I wonder if Bedstemor felt this same loss when we emigrated from Denmark.*

CHAPTER 79

Wendy had not been heard from in more than a year. In 1998, on the news, the Willy Pickton, pig farm, horror story was in the media. Many sex trade workers missing, and murdered. Kris thought of Wendy. The next day Aunt Elma called, "Kris, have you heard from Wendy or do you have contact information for her? She breezes in here once in a while unannounced when she visits friends out here on the Island. I started thinking about her last night as I watched the news."

"Oh, God, Elma, me too, the disgusting Pickton pig farm story, and the missing women got me thinking as well. I believe she is on the mainland but who knows with Wendy?"

Wendy surfaced at her aunt and uncle's home with her big dog, Elvis along. Aunt Elma was aware Wendy was in big trouble with drug and alcohol addiction. She contacted a rehab center and Wendy agreed to book into it at the end of the week.

She didn't follow through, but, took off and again was not heard from until a year later when she was hospitalized in White Rock, BC.

Kris happened to be visiting her family in BC and a call came there. Wendy knew how to contact Kari. Kris made the trip to visit her at the hospital.

"Wendy, why are you in here?" Kris asked while she watched her younger sister playing with rocks, glue and paint.

"Oh I have been staying on this farm with a bunch of friends. One of the girls' fathers owns the place. He loves my Elvis. He saw I was in pain, my stomach and legs swollen. He promised to care for Elvis if I would let him take me to hospital."

"Is it your Hepatitis C or the Cirrhosis of your liver that is causing this?"

"Who knows, I'm clean. I'm not using—just need a cigarette, damn I need a cigarette."

The unit nurse came and asked to speak with Kris in private, "Is there any family who will take Wendy in and help her with rehab?"

"No, absolutely not, Wendy is an adult even though she acts childlike. The system will have to support her. I know there are women's shelters, counseling and more. The times any family has helped her in the past turns into an enabling situation, and she knows how to twist it, and take adage."

"Well she can't stay here. She has health concerns but nothing can be done for her, and just to let you know she is still using. It is not my place to tell you but I heard her claiming to be clean. There was cannabis, cocaine, crystal meth in her blood work. I overheard her lies. I am not really allowed to say but you need to know."

"It does not surprise me in the least. Wendy has always been the queen of lies."

"Well, we will hook Wendy up with welfare, a women's shelter and a case worker then it's up to her what she does with the opportunity."

"Thank you for this meeting. I will talk about it with Wendy and encourage her to reach for a better life.

*****

When Kris was back at home, Wendy called in a hyper aggravated state, "Kris, I am out of hospital. I need cash. You have to wire me some cash.

"Are you not staying with the system as we discussed?"

"I can't, I have Elvis. He is not allowed. I am going back to the farm. Kris you have to send me money." Kris knew how the money would be used. *Damn it, tough love again.*

"No, Wendy, no money not now, not ever. Kari shopped for you and brought you better and warmer clothing. It was a gift and you are welcome but no cash Wendy!"

"You fucking bitch, I hate you!" Wendy the phone down and Kris never heard her spoken voice again.

One year passed. An evening phone call was answered by Kris, "Hello."

"Hello, Kirsten, I got your name and telephone number from a relative of yours in BC. I am a pastor from a church in Invermere, BC. I am calling about your sister, Wendy. She is in hospital in Calgary."

"She has been part of our congregation for almost a year now. I think she is very ill and thought you would want to know."

"Yes, thank you, for calling me. I will call the hospital."

Kris didn't get much information from the hospital staff.

The following day, Ed and Kris drove to Calgary.

"Oh, Wendy does have family," said the staffer on the desk when they arrived at the ward, "she has been our little mystery girl. Wait here I will get someone to take you in."

A nurse, gowned up, instructed us to do the same, "I must prepare you before we go in. Wendy has suffered a major stroke. You may get upset by all the equipment we have her hooked to."

At the sight of Wendy, Kris had choked up a bit, "What is her prognosis, I guess she is in a coma?"

Just then a doctor came into the room, and after introductions were made he said, "I am sorry to inform you, Wendy has no brain activity at all. She is on full life support. We have been waiting for family to make the decision to turn it off."

"This is a shock, well maybe not," Kris faltered, "Will any part of her body be usable for transplant?" *I must sound callous, I'm not falling apart. I should be emotional.*

"She has Hepatitis C, and Cirrhosis of the liver. If patients with those conditions need anything, then maybe, but not likely," replied the doctor.

None of her tissues were viable, Kris was informed later. *My baby sister gone at age 43.*

A memorial was held at the church Wendy frequented in her last year. Members of the congregation shared stories with kindness. There had been promise shown by Wendy to rehabilitate and live her life as a good Christian. One couple had taken her in to their home, and when she stayed there she did well but then the drug dealing abusive boyfriend, considered to be her common-law husband would show up and then she relapsed. The congregation had high hopes she would conquer. They were saddened by her passing.

That piece of scum, Billy showed up at the memorial, late, and under influence of substance. Kris felt like she wanted to rip his face off. But, no, it was not her way, she just stared him down with imaginary daggers flying through the air.

The pastor and his wife handed over card board boxes of the few belongings Wendy managed to keep from her chaotic life. The piece of scum took his pick. Kris put the boxes in the back of her car for perusal in private before disposal.

Much later the same evening, Kris began investigating items in the boxes. There were small painted rocks, dirty old make-up, hair bands and pony tail elastics, and broken short pencils, and some water paints. All of these were trash.

Wendy had shown an aptitude as an artist. Various drawings, sketches etc. held Kris' attention. There were notes, difficult to decipher and others written when she must have been lucid enough to make sense. Kris learned more about Wendy's life, from the diary Wendy kept. It seemed it was started after her involvement with the church. It was more than she wanted to know. *But this, all of this, from the start of 'Not to Talk About', to the end— When I feel I am all talked out, this will be included at the end of my own story. We were children in the same home affected by alcohol abuse and other dysfunctions.*

According to my psychologist we exhibited the four personalities among us (the need to fix and nurture, angry and abusive, comedic and in denial, addicted and criminal behavior) all a result of that toxic influence. These traits may be manifested in any number of children from an only child to several. It may help someone/anyone to parent. It is my fervent hope it may provide a strong reason to say NO TO SUBSTANCE ABUSE!

CHAPTER 80
DENMARK

November 2011, and she paused a moment. The door back then, was varnished and shiny, now it wore a thin coat of white paint. *Perhaps it is a base coat and a makeover is in progress.* She rang the bell and waited with confidence. Her father, CC, opened the door with a smile, "Welcome, come in," they shook hands. Ruth and Kirsten shared a strong hug, and Ruth said, "Welcome Kirsten, I am so happy you could come. Please take a seat, the tea is almost ready. Visit while I get it."

The coffee table was set with fine china on an embroidered cloth. Kirsten smiled at CC as she paid attention to the room, furnished and arranged the same. Ruth presented tea and a plate of buttered buns and cookies and said to Christian, "Can you manage the heavy tea pot and pour for us please?"

"I can," with trembling hands he managed the task.

Kirsten wondered when to seize the right moment to say what was in her heart. She turned to face Christian wanting him to know she was addressing him directly.

"Today I think of the day when first we met, right here, same seating, and drinking tea."

"Yes we are making it quite a habit," he said.

"The difference now is Ruth has joined us and that makes me happy," Kirsten smiled in Ruth's direction whose eyes filled with tears.

"I am so happy to know you and sorry I was unable to accept you then," said Ruth.

Kirsten needed to keep on with her rehearsed speech and looked directly at her father.

"Back then I came to meet you. Today I am here to say good bye, to you. I want to express my joy and gratitude towards you and your family for acceptance. I feel welcome and a part of all of you. The other night at the family dinner party there were memorable moments. When I entered the room and you rose from your chair, arms reaching, you asked if I was for sure your own little daughter. I hugged you and said with pride, yes I am. The times we have spent together will forever be among my greatest treasured memories"!

"When Palle, your son, asked my husband to move chairs so he could sit beside his sister and get to know her better, I was floored by the impact the word sister had on me. He put his arms around me, gave me a squeeze and a kiss on the cheek—so good and appreciated by me."

CC had a saddened look on his face, "I am happy you enjoyed it. Too bad we were not invited." Ruth and Kirsten shared a look.

"Are you really my son's sister?" Christian asked

"Yes I am, well, half-sister is more correct."

"Who is your father?" he asked. Ruth and Kirsten shared another look.

"You are my father," Kirsten answered.

"I am? No wonder you look handsome," CC smiled at her and continued "Who is your mother?"

"You were with her a short time, not a long time. Her name was Ava."

"Oh, yes, Ava, I know Ava," his voice became strong, almost angry.

Ruth coughed and said, "Shush, now be nice."

The visit lasted about an hour then Kirsten took the lead, "this is difficult for me. If I sit another ten minutes it won't be any easier. I am going to stand up and say good bye."

Christian rose up, unsteady. Kirsten took him in her arms, letting her tears trickle and said, "Thank you, so much, good bye."

Ruth fought her own tears, and joined the two of them and shared in a group hug. They followed her to the door. Kirsten turned to look back and saw the double doors swing shut.

I am fortunate I have fulfilled my dream. I found a big part of myself in him. I am sad to see him lost in his mind.

Kirsten Marie Wohlgemuth

INTRODUCING WENDY

Wendy was born April 24, 1963 in Calgary, Alberta. Her strongest recollections included such favorite thoughts as taking tap dancing, of her lovable toy monkey, and about her older brother, Karl. Her fondest memories were camping trips, the visits to her uncle's farm and cabin. Wendy could almost hear the sounds when she thought of the ice cream truck's music as it rolled through their neighborhood. Her favorite times in the year were spring, then snow and Christmas traditions with rice pudding and a hidden almond. Birthdays ranked high right up there, including the doll in a bottle, she once received. Wendy experienced Sunday school and the Bible for a short while during her formative years.

This is from her Diary compiled and edited by sister, Kirsten Marie Wohlgemuth

WENDY T. WITH A DOG NAMED ELVIS
I know my family came to Canada to start new in a new country, with many differences, especially a new language. It was hard for them and a new baby was not in their plan. They were often thought of as my grandparents. I was the only Canadian born in our family and without a middle name I was somewhat different from the rest. I remember a lot from when I was young, such as Kris, my oldest sister was like my second mom. She was my caregiver a lot until I started school. I don't remember much of my brother

Karl living at home, besides my dad, Karl was also my hero.

I remember my mother.

I knew who my dad was. A tall man who could make me be shy, except on allowance day when I wanted to collect. In grade 2, I got a dime. When I got that dime, I spent that dime fast. One of my fondest memories was the day my friends were going to the store. I already spent my dime. I took myself into the house and called dad. He stood tall, intimidating, and high above me at the top of the stairs.

Too late to change my mind, I said "Dad, I know I spent my dime already but may I please have another dime to go with the neighbor kids to the store?" And, by the grace of God, he flipped me another dime. I felt the guy was out of this world.

Camping, lots of it, in a station wagon and a tent trailer at Lake Louise and other places such as the Calgary Zoo and Drumheller. It seems like it was to go on forever. I wanted to be a baton twirler and win trophies. Baton in hand, too young to get it, but I was determined to be good.

One day I remember my dad coming home from the hospital after he his foot was amputated. Coming up the back stairs, he stepped down as if he forgot he had no foot. This was the beginning of my Dad's nightmare. They ended up taking another portion off his leg. Losing his legs led to heavy drinking. He had poor circulation and he got gangrene. They gave him whiskey in the hospital to *thin his blood. I think he may have thought this would save his life. He smoked till the day he died. We ended up moving to Victoria as a result, to get away from snow etc. and to make it easier for dad in a warmer climate. We left for Victoria with the station wagon and the tent trailer. My brother Karl joined us later. Moving to Victoria was the start of me bonding with my dad.*

Fishing--he'd take me fishing with him, not for my company but for more fish. We went all the time until they ended up buying a Laundromat and dry cleaning business-and my sneaky ways began. I spent a lot of time at the Laundromat, a left alone operator. My dad would leave me there as he went for lunch. I was supposed to give change to customers. I gave change all right–right into my own pocket. Dad caught on and set me up. I was caught. When I was in grade 2, I got caught stealing a bra at the Fields store and later stealing rubber cement glue to make rubber balls. Early in my life, I felt I was already failing my father

I had two friends, Brenda and Louise. They had a handicapped brother, Ernie. He and I shared the same birthday. I was his only friend. Our house had a separate entrance to the basement where I used to play. Ernie would sneak over to see me–he knew I was his friend. One day, my Mom was in the basement, and when Ernie appeared she chased him out with a broom. I witnessed several inhuman acts against Ernie even by his own family. One day I got news my special friend was dead. Kids threw rocks at him, and he ran into a back yard, three doors down, locked him-self in a fridge. My friend was gone forever.

At school I sat on the steps crying for Ernie. Many, including his sister, made fun about his death and my tears for him. I was devastated–I spoke to him daily.

Shortly after this sad time, just after crossing the tracks during my trip to the store a car pulled up with two men in it. One jumped out, naked, and he yelled 'kill her.' I ran to a house, a lady took me in. Five minutes later one of the two men walked through the door. I freaked and accused him–he denied. I was too scared to tell my parents.

Two days later I was walking to Ernie's house to see his sisters. I spent quite a lot of time there. They lived across the road beside the house where I ran to and where I believed the naked man lived. I saw the man in their back yard with their rabbits. He looked at me, and I looked at him. Right in front of me he picked up a rabbit, wrung its neck, and shook it towards me as if he would do the same to me.

Panicked, I ran into my friends' house without knocking. I flew in the door, huffing and puffing slamming the door shut behind me. They looked at me, puzzled. I did not tell. I apologized for not knocking. I never told another soul about it. I thought I could not tell. I would not be let out again because they would be mad at me for it happening to me.

I remember the camping we did. We camped with my sister, Kris and my brother in law, Ed and my niece and nephew Kari and Dean. They lived in a little community, a hamlet, known as Wildwood, Alberta.

One of my dad's brothers of five, Uncle Ben and my Auntie Elma moved to BC and bought a Motel there after owning hotels in Alberta. They had three kids, Marion, Karina, and Doug. That's it—all of my family as it consists in Canada. Their move was a big thing.

I am reminded of my grandmother, my dad's mom. She visited us in Victoria and then she was to fly to Calgary to visit her son, Ben and his family, in which ever hotel they owned at the time. I went with her—my first flight, lasting 1 hour and some minutes. My Bedstemor spoke no English-oh boy! Nervously I watched the clock, thinking as long as it was only a 1-hour flight. Everyone must know what it is to watch a clock. Everyone must have done it some time. Off we go, this big Danish woman who knows no English. We can't even communicate. I am feeling a wee bit intimidated. It was a lunch flight. When lunch came it included a huge peach or nectarine which I was looking forward to eating. When Bedstemor snatched it from my tray and placed it deep down, in her bag, I was shocked. Did she really take my peach away from me? Uncle Ben picked us up and then there was what seemed a long drive for me as the elders caught up, speaking only Danish, Ja! We pulled up to the hotel and Oh Boy! I meet my cousins once again. Before hotels they lived on a farm. I always loved visiting them. My Auntie Elma was my favorite, so kind. She never drinks. She sure puts up with a whole lot of drunken Dane-Vikings with horns.

I thought how cool it was we kids could go to the restaurant and order lunch and ice cream. Afterwards, grandmother, uncle, auntie, cousins and I were off to their cabin at Sylvan Lake, just outside Red Deer. I was excited, my sister Kris and Ed, Kari and Dean and my mom and dad. This was the beginning of many reunions minus relatives in Denmark. After the lake I went with Kris and Ed to the little town, Wildwood, which would be my summer home for many years to come. I loved every minute I spent there. I met my first boyfriend there, a boy I still think of to this day. God, bless him!

*****

In 1972 I failed grade two. When I went in to grade three, I remember I had a boy haircut. We moved to Langford where mom and dad lived until dad died. I met Candi, Maria, and Carol. From grade three and on life was more or less the same from year to year but I came out of my shell and developed a hard side. No one 'Fucked' with Wendy T! This is something I regret to this day. I am not proud of it for sure! For example, in grade 3, I called out a grade seven boy, a hall monitor. This was my first ever real physical fight and boy was I scared! In grade four and five, I liked playing kissing tag. I felt I knew everything by now. I had fun raiding gardens with Jim and Kevin. By the time I was in grade eight things were not going at all well for my mom and dad. I was left alone a lot with a lot of strict rules. The only good thing for me was my involvement with sports, namely Lacrosse and a Baton course. Actually in grades six, seven and some of grade 8, I was way out of control with teachers and school. I was on a kind of mission from Hell. I sniffed glue, started smoking cigarettes and pot, and alcohol became a great thing. I stole my mother's jewelry, and I lied a lot. I hitchhiked up Island with friends.

Each Friday night I went skating. My dad drove my friend and me and picked us up. We were drunk every time but dad never said anything. Saturday nights it was the speedway and afterwards it was the Bush Bunny Hardy Party. I had my second boyfriend but he did not last long as he made his way around afterwards. I always stayed at my girlfriend's house. By grade eight, school was a subject I hated. All I wanted to do was skip out and party and why not, everyone else was doing it? Mom and dad were always at work. Because my mom's English was not too good I would just write a note and she would sign it. My best homework was mastering her signature down pat. When the notes were coming in almost every day, I got caught. When I was in grade nine it was either, I quit or I would get expelled from school district 62.

My dad was devastated, his hurt and anger was worse even than when I stole the car, dented it, and on and on. But, when things happened, it was never talked about again.

*****

I remember a family Christmas breaking into a big fight. With drinks came fights. I remember fights about me like it was yesterday. I can still hear 'I am taking Wendy, no we are taking Wendy.' Wendy, Wendy, Wendy...later it was 'Wendy is this Wendy is that.' Wendy, Wendy, Wendy...

Back to the Island I go and I can still hear my dad say, 'What are we going to do with you?' A couple of weeks went by and then off partying again. I sort of got back with my second boyfriend, Jeff. I slept with him–my first time. By now my mom and dad asked me if I would go live at my Brother Karl's place and take a hairdressing course. Kris was a hairdresser. I always looked up to her. I held her high and I said Okay, and was off to Stony Plain, Alberta to live with Karl and his wife, Laura.

I was ready to start my course in Edmonton but about a week or two before start day I missed my period. I was seventeen and pregnant. I was asked if I wanted to have it but I knew dad would be devastated if I kept it and I was still on their medical. I was flown back to the Island and dad drove me to the hospital the next morning for my abortion, and he said, 'I'll be back to pick you up.' Nothing was said then nor ever even mentioned again. Back I fly to Edmonton.

*****

My brother was a true Viking drinker who allowed the booze to take over his life as it did to most of my family. My brother was an Ironworker, a BIG strong guy. His wife worked as a church secretary but did not practice religion. She had two kids whom I became big sister and babysitter to. I started my hairdressing course and Friday nights I babysat. Each night, I played backgammon with Karl and Laura, their favorite game. We played for hours, drinking a lot. They had a dog, the poor thing, suffered terrible abuse when my brother's bad temper exploded. It was too awful for me to go into detail about. My brother always seemed mad.

I met a girl named Pam, with a gold Trans Am. Lover Boy was the tape and party hardy was our way. We frequented taverns and house parties, out of control. Still I always passed every written test and I caught on quickly to cutting hair. My sister Kris took me to Hair Shows. She owned her own salon in Wildwood. I went, hung over as usual.

After I was 900 hours into my course, the school celebrated with a baseball game and a party. A girl from school drove me. I was nearly passed out but I do know a bus drove right in front of us. My arm went up, smack! Next I remember Jaws of Life, the cutting of my clothes, and no water. I was hopping

283

mad–I didn't care about injuries. My knee was wide open and my forehead was split in half so to speak! I was in hospital for a week and a bit. Hell, I wanted out. I did not want to miss anything and so every second stitch taken out, I left. I went to Wildwood but my interest was not Kris and her family. It was in leaving out the back door. I went with my first boyfriend, and went horseback-riding. When I returned to my brother's we had a 'Big One'. He kicked me out.

Mom and dad paid for an apartment I was sharing with Hughy. A guy I knew from Langford and a longtime friend. I kicked him out because he ate my food. What a Bitch I was.

I started seeing a guy from the bar I liked to frequent. There were warrants out for his arrest. His van was left at my place and his family got hold of me to get it. I went to his court date, and met his parents. I was at the time staying with a friend as my rent money was stolen. His parents asked me to move in with them while he did his time. God I really can't remember his name but I think he got six months.

I moved in with his parents in Leduc. They were a born-again Christian family. This was my first encounter with The Lord. This brought me to be baptized in the Holy Spirit and blessed in Tongue. I lived there three months went through two jobs. He got out. He hit me. I phoned Kris, she came to get me out of there.

I moved to Red Deer, and stayed with my cousin Marion and Bud. I got a job, lost it–sexual harassment. I moved in with a couple, they got kicked out of their place. Mom and dad came to Sylvan Lake cabin and took me back to Langford. I got ten grand from the accident, blown in three months.

I lived with Randy who got me on cocaine and then the needle. He beat me, he left. I was pregnant, but, I aborted. I got a criminal charge and had to do community service at the fairgrounds where I met a Carny, hot- hot. He beat up Randy.

Then I was with Les, a real space monkey, who got chased out of town by bikers. He was heading to Ontario but his motor running without oil, ceased somewhere around Calgary. Cops came along and arrested Les on outstanding warrants. I was left to rot with Sinbad, an old neighbor, and a cabby.

I stayed with a girlfriend and Steven. I visited Les in the city cells and I started selling acid and pot. I was charged and jailed fifteen days. Then partying, selling, partying, and then Les got out. He cheated on me, and I left him.

I took a train to Vancouver with two friends. I lost Sinbad–sad, sad, sad. I moved in with big time dealers–now the real fun began. May God have Mercy on my soul!

In West Vancouver I immediately met my new friends/family: Michelle, Reco, John, Mark, and Greg. Michelle already claimed Gregg, later a few more.

For now I was a hit with my new friends. They accepted me right away, and they were going to show me the ropes, and give me tips on selling pot and acid on Granville. The block, from McDonalds to end of The Bay was our turf. Good money, one quarter of pot I'd get 14 grams, go figure. I was doubling my money plus some. On a welfare day I would turn it over three to five times in one day maybe two. A check back then was only two almost three hundred a day, working four to six hours per day.

We all looked out for each other when police were near. Someone would alert us all by yelling 'six,' then we would vanish into thin air. For the first year police never knew me or saw me.

If you play a game, you play and win. After selling we would go for a couple of drinks then head home. The guys had their place and Michelle and I had ours. We partied until all hours of the night. First I started to see Mark with the blond hair and sweet look. He went to Ontario for a month, Reco and I hooked up. I broke Mark's heart. Reco was a real ladies man. I knew Joe liked me from the start but I could not commit. I played all three. Never was I been that easy but it was on my terms when and with whom. I decided. If I lusted after someone, I'd hustle him but if they liked me too much, wanting to be more serious, I would instantly hate them.

Relationships never lasted past a year. I would start fights for no reason to let them go. I broke hearts. They never broke mine. What a hard soul I was. But, my new family accepted me for me, no matter what.

Shayna started coming around, never lived with us. I will call her a native beauty.
She was a tall confident person who took no shit, just like the rest of us. For some reason she watched over me like I was breakable. They introduced me to MDA, the love drug, strobe ninety. I loved it. Partying was our life. We were making money and we were never without drugs. We were big time spenders or so we thought. After a year of selling drugs on Granville unseen by cops, I began getting sloppy after all the drugs and booze. We were at our extreme–drugs, sex, and rock and roll. We didn't care about nothing.

Shayna and I were drunk after a wake for our good friend, Trigger who died when he crashed his motor bike. We drank a 40 of Scotch, Trigger's favorite. We were on Granville, (called Granville Island?)and stopped at a little 'Packie' shop where we got into an argument with the clerk. We ripped his shop to pieces. We broke everything in it and the big window too. Going out towards our waiting cab, we saw a paddy wagon and cops. In no time we are down on the ground. Shayna had a foot on her back by her neck. She tried to lift her head but it was smashed into the ground. I was slammed up against the paddy wagon. We were cuffed and off to city cells we went–wee what a ride. They threw us around like puppets, smashed our heads, first on one side then on the other side, smashed us to the floor, our bodies and faces were bruised up good. Booked and celled we wanted our pictures taken and demanded to see a judge in the morning. Shayna's face was messed up good. Lo and behold they kicked us out at two in the morning, with a court date two months away, not the next morning. Sneaky bad boys, those cops were this way, no proof. Here we are on the deserted street, and flagged down a taxi, hopped in. It was the same cab we got pulled out of at the 'Packie' shop.

I landed two assaults, three trafficking, three possessions, three failing to appear, three failing to comply with court order, and three mischiefs. Life was not good. Our street family was falling apart. At the same time I met Ralph and JD. They were hippie like, how did they become my best friends? Well, for MDA, which they sold, I learned how to sell MDA. JD was house mom, and took care of everything. I made a big mistake. He hid the MDA downstairs where I slept, and I accidentally saw—I helped myself. I would sell it at my new bar, pot as well. I was dropping it every day.

One day I had enough and I moved back to Victoria but with DA on hand. I had warrants coming out of my Ying yang and a girl who hated me turned me in. The cops picked me up. I tried passing off my stolen ID–my alias, Lisa Myers. I defrauded Welfare with her name for two years. The police challenged me and took me to the station. In the car I go. They lifted the back seat then sat me down. Inside I was *carrying 4 grams of DA wrapped separately. I put them under their seat. They pulled out a file and I admitted to being Wendy T–no dog named Elvis yet. I was charged with impersonation, fraud, and possession of stolen property. In the morning they drove me downtown Victoria to the city cells. I stayed there until court. I stood, looking like hell in the criminal booth. The list of charges against me piled up. I plead guilty. The judge said this was a perfect example of the courts being too lenient to people like me. One year, and nine months–Oh my god! I started adding them up, concurrent what does it mean?*

I was handcuffed, on a six seat plane, flying over the ocean, not happy. Off to Okalala jail. like jails on TV right down to debugging with spray, bend over, the whole nine yards. Two East Indians came in the same time. Oh my word they already knew we were coming. All the rooms wanted and argued about getting me. In the morning they assigned me to kitchen duties, three bucks a day. I had just started in, and five minutes at this job when I was pulled out for classification. I was twenty five years old. I was approved to go to the farm. Only one night in Okalala, Praise God!

This place was beautiful–tennis court, huge field, big rooms, TV room, ceramic hut, huge green house, and a chicken farm. I did four months out of my time. Some of this was at a sewing barn. They sewed all the jeans for all jails across Canada. We were a little mean. We packaged them, and we would sew one leg shut, maybe sew 'fag' on the back pocket and send dirty notes. I sewed for one week, and then applied for the outside maintenance job. I drove a John Deer tractor for the rest of the time. They also had a Day Care center.

They supplied Okalala and a few other places with eggs. The warden would ask me to wash her car all the time. I detailed it for her. She liked me. I cut hair for smokes and candy, and I painted on ceramics. I worked one hour at the Day Care at noon. I painted fences at the playground, I was a hit. The grounds never looked so good.

When I went in front of the parole board I felt sick, I knew I didn't get parole. I came out a wreck. To my surprise the warden and my case manager went to talk to them. They pretty much gave their right foot for me. APPROVED! I was out of there. Mrs. Drew, the warden praised my work around there,

Candi, my best friend picked me up, and we went straight to the beer store. She drove me to the ferry, drunk. On the way home she smashed up her truck. I was off to a good start.

My goal when I got out was to finish my hairdressing course, which I succeeded in doing even though I was either drunk or hung over. I moved in with a family with three kids whom I lived with off and on for years to come. It was then I met Don who went by nickname of Crank. We moved up to Duncan. He seemed to have it together. He was a heavy-duty mechanic and owned a 32 foot cabin cruiser and was nice as pie. We went on holiday together, first to my sister Kris'. I was bored then. They were always working and didn't want to go bar hopping, but he met my family, and I think they liked him. He already met mom and dad. Then we were off to Grande Prairie to meet part of his family who all lived on farms. Then we were off to Mackenzie where we were married at Lions Lake. There were just the two of us, with one of his brothers and a sister in law standing up for us. My secret—I only married to get it over with, get respectable. When his year was up, I left.

I got a job with a longtime friend, Brian, who knew me growing up. Brian had a misfortune and became a quadriplegic. I would do his personal care, his house and his yard. This was a live in position, three days on and three days off. It started my job with Independent Living. I lived with five residents. One was blind, a Jerry Lewis look alike with Great Spirit for life. He loved to play DJ and had a huge collection of records in boxes, which I was not to touch. He knew where to find every record in any of the boxes.

There was a girl with brain injury, stubborn and demanding who soon moved out, to get her own place. A guy two feet tall took her place and he lusted after me 24 hours a day, no... way! Another fella with MS stayed in his smelly room, feeling sorry for himself and drinking.

One of my clients, Harvey and I became best of friends, stuck like glue. One day I took him home with me, we got him upstairs and that was that, he wasn't going back to the group home. I quit the home and we got a place suitable for his needs. My dad rigged up a shower and whatever else was needed. My dad could do and fix anything. Harvey and I drank a lot and we enjoyed riding all over Langford, me on the back of his chair and Pudge, my Maltie-poo on his knee. Drunk or not, in about 3 months we got our way and were approved for me to get paid for Harvey's care.

The same day we went for a drive in Harvey's van and I smashed into a car carrier. Harvey flew from his wheel chair, over the front seat and was jammed. I was in pain with broken thumb bones. Harvey could not move and he was scared and in pain. Even though he was paralyzed he still felt pain. I was devastated, feeling like the biggest looser ever. He was hospitalized, no more Independent Living

*****

I dated Dave, a real looker with a steady job. He didn't like my excessive drinking. I became pregnant. I miscarried. A month later I was pregnant again with a tubal pregnancy, which almost cost me my life. I just drank more and Dave dumped me. For the first time I was dumped. Even though it hurt I got over it fast.

I made plans to move to the main land and live with my friend Candi. We were friends since grade three. She lived in Maple Ridge. Mom and dad were going to drive me. I was excited about this and looked forward to this ride with my mom and dad.

The night before, we were sitting around the kitchen drinking 'The Vikings poison' Rye.

My dad and I started fighting. I don't remember what about. It got physical. My dad was out of his wheel chair, on the floor. He had been in a chair for years. He did not like his phony legs. They caused sores, a chance of more gangrene. I spent a lot of time helping and learning from my dad. I loved him and needed his approval. He picked himself up into his chair called my mom. They took their puppy and left the house. I was devastated once again. They stayed at a motel and came home early the next morning without a glance or word for me–no ride for me. I went to our neighbors, Bob and Janice. Bob gave me a ride and Candi picked me up at the Ferry.

Two weeks later, Janice called to tell me dad was dead. My little dog, Pudge and I were on the next ferry. My niece, Kari, Uncle Ben, Aunt Elma were there and soon my brother, sister, Ed and Dean arrived. The day of dad's funeral I was locked up inside myself. My brother, I think took it the worst. That night we were getting ready–all of us were to go to the Princess Mary for Dinner. My brother in law came up to me and cold as ice he said, "Wendy, we know you think it's your fault but it isn't. We are all going to Princess Mary and you are more than welcome to join us if you want to." Talk about being put on the spot with a sword in my heart. From that day on, all of them were never the same to me, except for my brother. They were with him, my dad.

Within that year my mom had a stroke. My sister, Kris, whisked her up, flew her to Red Deer, and put her in a nursing home. She sold the house and kicked my ass to the curb–left me standing without my family or a home.

*****

I had Bob and Janice. We were real close.

I made a call to Crank, and he came from Mackenzie the next day and moved me up there.

I left him for a mountain man, a real sicko. We lived in the bush for a couple of years in a cabin the size of a closet, just outside Clinton. When I moved back to Maple Ridge, I began my journey with the Bible.

###

At this point in the diary, several pages had been torn out. What was in those pages? Could it have been about her relationship with Ava? Did she write something she regretted? Kris still wonders but she will never know.

###

Dear God thanks for giving your only son for me. I ask for forgiveness again and again, only to sin again and again. I take full responsibility for my own actions. I am sick and as far as I know no one close to me cares. I feel like every wrong thing in their lives is my doing. I pray, from my whole being, Billy's mom will suffer no more, thinking I am not with him, which is a lie. I don't think anyone else has as much hate for me as she does. I pray to God for her and her whole family. I pray for my family, who I know, thinks I'm a lost cause just like Karl. Karl, I love you, miss you, and I think I understand your feelings. I feel the same way. I'll tough it out for the both of us. Please God, take care of him.

Daddy, I'm sorry, I love you and all my life I wanted you to like me, silly, I know you loved me. Mom, I hurt all of you. Please forgive me, I love you and Kris must be right—I was just out to see what I could get. I have been in denial but I think that I thought I was looking for love and acceptance of my life in my fun place and the way I think. The thought is we are here for a reason only God knows.

Jesus, Billy needs peace now. I pray you forgive us for being so nasty. Help us all to sleep sound. I ask you to send more of those dreams that come to me and give me a sign. Be it you dad, I felt your presence. Karl did you hold my hand that one night? Did you speak to my friend? Mom you are with both your sons now. God bless you, Karl, and Kaj! Amen!

Help me find the way to be strong and fight off mine and the Devil's habits that tempt me day in and out, In Jesus' name, Wendy T.

I still must talk and deal with it. Today I found out my long time partner's mom is on her deathbed, five days give or take a few to live. Now this woman hates me like I've never been hated before. She again blames me for everything wrong in their family's life, things that happened way before I knew them but it was still my fault. When I got sick, she would say awful things like 'die, then you will be out of our life.' When my brother shot himself, she said 'Why don't you kill yourself, like your brother did?'

I forgave her. I stopped going over to her house and became invisible to her and their family. She was sick with cancer. Out of respect I did not want to add to her stress, she already knew she was dying and I'm hurting again not able to give support or love in her death or ever finding out why she hated me. She hates me like no other and there will be no amends. Again another life ends and I'm hurt again. May God have mercy on her soul and may she rest in peace. The war is over.

Year after year after year my wild ways took effect on the people who mattered, the most to me. Year after year I didn't get what they saw. I thought I was okay, happy go lucky, giving everything—for a reason I didn't see.

It was always a blur. My family was small and dying before I could change. I began running more away from myself. Every so often I would hear 'Wendy Witch' in fact God was calling on me but I wasn't ready. I continued until my drinking caught up to me. My liver was done but the devil cocaine Ja, it still played the game. Bottom line is I hurt not only mom, dad, or brother, I hurt myself. Forgive me for my words that hurt someone. Forgive me for I have my brother's temper. I am sorry and take full responsibility, pointing no fingers, for God has given me a second chance, which I'm holding on to.

The Good Bye Valley–Billy
Our time together has come to an end. We both know this as hard as it is. I gave you your last chance, coming to Invermere. From day one you lied, about what? Well drugs–I let it all ride for the drugs. They were always there. They were my friends, my company, and my everything. No problem getting them, you put them in front of my face every day. As days lingered on, it got worse. Things, you said and did was all against me. Your controlling, jealous rages, against me–the accusations and stories, in my eyes, were your own guilt, such as when Berta and her friend were in my house, cranking with you. That was A Okay. But, if I was having a conversation with anyone, even 67 year-old, Horst, according to you I was blowing or laying him–right down to my pastor. Sick you are! Sick I am, my liver's done, and my life with you will kill me. You are an actor Billy, and a good one. People don't see it. They side with you and I become the reason for everyone's downfall, with your intimidating ways, you have the world fooled. For many years I've had you pegged. Right now

you're out of your mind–mad—because Billy, you can't accept the truth. I've taken responsibility for my take in everything and I'm taking action to better myself. I'm not going to die until God says. I am going to make it. What I see for myself to come is the best for Elvis and me.

As much as you say you'll change for me is why we have no future. You Billy, have to want to change. In order to do this change you must admit fully– you have a problem.

I'm not going back. I'm going forward, straight ahead to the little light of my church and everything it stands for. These are things that don't include you.

The future is Elvis' and mine, right now. I must stay focused, my life depends on it. Something I and only I can do. I need time to truly find myself. My whole life, I've lived for everyone else. Here on in, I'm living for myself and God. For the first time I will become whole in the person I am. If you are hurt and angry over my decision to move on, I'm sorry. Hurt is something I don't wish for you. There's someone out there that can fill your need right down to sex, which I can't give anymore, to you or anyone else for that matter. Please accept and respect my decision and move on to a better you as I am with myself. I am a child of God with a dog named Elvis. Thanks for the little good and I am sorry for all that was bad. I'll pray for you in my new being. But I have to say Good Bye!

To My Addictions (psalm 102)
We played a game with your rules and we played for many, many years till my days have been consumed in smoke and my bones have been scorched like a hearth. My heart has been smitten, like grass it has withered away. I forget to eat my bread because of the loudness of my groaning. My bones cling to my flesh. I resemble a pelican of the wilderness. I have become like an owl of the waste palaces. I lie, awake, and have become like a lonely bird on a housetop. Know this game is old and now the rules have changed.

We're done, finished. You lose. We can't start over for your rules I have handed over to Jesus and he to God. I win, game over. Beat that!

*****

What a day my liver is hurting me, my stomach is extended and I'm uncomfortable, same pain. Went to the clinic—extended liver, hurts so, and measured 33 inches.

Oh God, I am hungry and anxious for you to welcome me to your castle. You've been calling me for a long time. I know it's time to say goodbye to all sins. I hear my dog cry every night for I've let him down too. Help me now, I can't wait no longer, I must make it right, can't go on with no sleep or food. I feel sick and dirty, my teeth feel like sandpaper, my skin is crawling, and my hair is dull. I hate what I see. I am dying. I hurt from head to toe and in my brain. I don't

NOT TO TALK ABOUT—UNTIL NOW

want this sadness I feel every day. I'm useless and I sit with no future. I need you, oh God, take my hand, I reach for you with all my will. Please God, today, not tomorrow for tomorrow is too late. I must go today. Lift me up, oh God, I am ready. I want my grass greener my garden full. Cleanse me from all evil and stop my wandering eyes so they stay focused on you and only you, oh God! Thank you, oh, God, I see the light, it's bright!

*****

July 9, 2006 Wendy was charged with 'Assault with a weapon' (a knife) towards Billy and she signed same document on July 10, 2006. Wendy was to appear in court on Sept 26, 2006, five days after her death

She died of a massive stroke at age 43, the same age Karl was when he died.

Wendy left several notations about her condition of Hepatitis C, Cirrhosis of the liver, drug use etc., and about the symptoms, and treatments, life style etc. Among all of the papers there were several worthy and talented pencil sketches.

Kris and Wendy lived their lives different from one another, except one common denominator was— everything in their family was '*NOT TO TALK ABOUT.*'

Kris has struggled with this story she has felt the need to write before all of the events even happened. She has wished for a sibling relationship that could have and should have been very different.

Wendy did not complete the following poem. Kris assumed she wrote up to the minute she had the stroke.

THE DAY MY ANGEL CAME

The *day my angel came*
H*eat was high, more than the sun*
Each *leaf dying, but they weren't done*

D*ogs were restless, no cats around*
Anger *grow, voices drown*
Y *(why) so sad, came from a little frown*

M*y heart was pounding faster, faster*
You *want to go, he just got madder*

And *stopped over and over*
No *go he was m*
G *(just) let me go pound, pound my heart*
Ai
L

C

A

M

E

GOOD BYE LITTLE SISTER

39110191R00171

Made in the USA
Charleston, SC
25 February 2015